DEDICATION AND THANKS

TO THE GREATEST, WHO HAVE DARED TO TRAVEL THE PATHS OF THE MIND, OF THE HEART, OF ENERGY, OF THE QUANTUM FIELD, OF THE ASTRAL, OF OTHER PLANES THAT WE DO NOT SEE, ETC. WHATEVER WE CALL IT, THANKS TO THOSE WARRIORS FOR HAVING TRAVELLED THAT PATH, THAT WORLD THAT NOBODY SEES, BUT CAN BE PERCEIVED, FELT AND NOTICED....

IF ONE DAY THEY READ IT...

THANK YOU CORRADO MALANGA
THANK YOU EDUARDO COLETTO
THANK YOU JOE DISPENZA

AND OF COURSE, TO A VERY SPECIAL GIRL FOR ME, WHOM I HAVE LOVED MORE THAN ANY OTHER. ONE NIGHT, IN HER ROOM, LISTENING TO HER ATTENTIVELY, THE TWO OF US LYING DOWN, SHE TOLD ME TO THINK BIG, SOMETHING THAT WOULD REVOLUTIONISE THE WORLD ALREADY, AND MAKE IT BETTER. THAT I WOULD MAKE THE BEST BOOK IN THE WORLD FOCUSED ON CHANGING PEOPLE'S LIVES, A SERIOUS BOOK, WHICH WILL WAKE UP THE WHOLE OF HUMANITY VERY QUICKLY, A BOOK OF GOOD UNDERSTANDING, EFFECTIVE, SOMETHING NEVER SEEN BEFORE, WHICH WILL GENERATE A CHANGE IN THE CONSCIOUSNESS OF HUMANITY FOREVER AND THUS IMPROVE THE COLLECTIVE CONSCIOUSNESS AND THUS ALSO IMPROVE HUMAN RELATIONS. THIS BOOK IS DEDICATED TO ALL THOSE FAILED SOUL MATE RELATIONSHIPS THAT WE HAVE EXPERIENCED, BUT ABOVE ALL THAT WE NEVER WANTED TO BREAK OR DEGENERATE, BECAUSE WE REALLY KNEW THAT WE WERE LOVING EACH OTHER.
WE REALLY KNEW THAT WE WERE LOVING EACH OTHER IN EVERY WAY.

IF ONE DAY I READ IT...

THANK YOU RAQUEL MARTÍNEZ

Break Free from Intrusive Thoughts

Starting server ...

BREAK FREE FROM INTRUSIVE THOUGHTS

Pablo García (La Rioja)

Break Free from Intrusive Thoughts

Copyright © 2022

All right reserved.

CONTENT

INTRODUCTION

CHAPTER 1:	The Five Layers of Human Being	Pág.1
CHAPTER 2:	The Human Brain	Pág.12
CHAPTER 3:	The Etheric Contracts	Pág.23
CHAPTER 4:	The Intrusions	Pág.26
CHAPTER 5:	The Archons	Pág.30
CHAPTER 6:	The Lyonels	Pag.35
CHAPTER 7:	The Grays	Pag.39
CHAPTER 8:	The Reptiles	Pag.43
CHAPTER 9:	The Mantis	Pag.48
CHAPTER 10:	The Lux	Pag.49
CHAPTER 11:	The Clones and the Sheeple	Pag.50
CHAPTER 12:	Eliminate Fear	Pag.52
CHAPTER 13:	The Limiting Pattern and Arborescent Thinking	Pag.61
CHAPTER 14:	The "Energetic Punch" Drainages	Pag.64
CHAPTER 15:	Transmutation Techniques	Pag.67
CHAPTER 16:	The Avatar	Pag.69
CHAPTER 17:	The Time Master	Pag.75
CHAPTER 18:	The Powerfull Bear	Pag.77
CHAPTER 19:	Detect Healthy People and Toxic People	Pag.79
CHAPTER 20:	¿Why Don´t People Understand Each Other?	Pag.81
CHAPTER 21:	¿How to Fix Your Problems?	Pag.88
CHAPTER 22:	Final Words	Pag.93

INTRODUCTION

It is not easy to write a book, it takes a lot of time and a lot of mental energy. However, this is a very important topic for me and I want my eager readers to have the best. I'm going to be myself throughout this book but it is going to be very difficult to explain everything, and also challenging to assimilate this powerful information. That's why I'm asking you for patience. BUT I PROMISE THAT AFTER READING THIS BOOK, YOU WILL BE A COMPLETELY EMPOWERED BEING WHO CAN ACTIVATE THE ARBORESCENT THINKING WITHIN.

I'm just another human being on this planet just like you. I was born in 1987, in the city of Vitoria (EUSKADI – Basque Country), Spain on July 19th at 2 pm. This of course makes me a Gemini with Virgo in the ascendant according to the Zodiac.

Just like you, I went to a public elementary school and to a public high school. I sat on a square chair, at a square desk, in a square classroom, with some classmates who were also square-headed, and some square-headed teachers as well.

In my opinion, they should include basic subjects in the education system, such as:

- Vegetable patch skills to promote food self-sufficiency
- Medicinal plants
- Mixed martial arts
- Extreme survival skills and techniques
- Long-term memory reinforcement and speed-reading skills
- Psychology, neuroscience, and epigenetics
- Cold energy or free energy and energetic self-sufficiency
- Civics (e.g. the Constitution, civil code, penal laws)
- International Commercial Law, Admiralty Law and Maritime Law
- Sovereignty and Natural Law

Instead of the above-mentioned subjects, we have **all** been victims of social programming or social engineering, which has promoted competition with each other, instead of collaboration. In other words, competition has been a huge focus instead of a more humane education focusing on each of our strengths. Every year, in schools all around the world, the same subjects are taught. For example, when we think about mathematics, I'm sure that you have never used derivates, integrals, or square roots in your adult life.

When you really think about it, education is just programming us to fight amongst ourselves. They teach us how to read and add numbers so we can create and pay invoices in the future. Throughout this programming over our school life, they train us to treat the teacher figure as an authority figure, so we will be used to giving into the authority of state forces, like the Police.
Everything is focused on fear, stress, and obedience...

Break Free from Intrusive Thougts

This book wants to empower the individual to stop feeling afraid of not complying with this obedience.
I'm not seeking anarchy, but for real sovereignty within each of us.

1: THE FIVE LAYERS OF A HUMAN BEING

We will start from the easiest to the hardest, but first let's introduce them all:

- Physical body
- Mental body
- Emotional body
- Energetic body
- Spiritual body or spirit or infinite cosmic consciousness or light body

When we talk about the fifth layer, people always ask the difference between the soul and the spirit, or at least they are confused about it. This is something we will clarify further in the book.

I should also mention, the five layers must be followed in order because I can assure you from my own experience that if you don't know anything about your physical body, if you can't fully control it, being the easiest layer...your arms and legs for example... forget about starting up new neuronal circuits in your brain to deactivate the old ones. This being said, there is always an exception that proves the rule... and that breaks the rule. But really, this is something to seriously consider.

I want to make it clear that everything that happens in our body, either happens consciously or subconsciously. Let's look at some examples: If we want to raise our arm and we do it, that is a conscious movement. If we want to move a leg, we move it, and similarly if we want to open our mouth or move our eyebrows or our eyes, we just do it. All of these movements are conscious because we command them to be executed.
This of course makes sense, but there are also several unconscious executions happening in our physical body, like the beating of our humble heart to which we never pay attention and it goes unnoticed. Another clear example of the subconscious in our physical body is the digestion process; it is done and that's it, we are not commanding it in a conscious way, nor do we operate the expulsion of our gastric juices, it is done automatically. The same goes for wound healing or the nine months during pregnancy.

It is very important to consider that there will always be a conscious and a subconscious mind, that is to say, there will always be actions that we do ourselves and others that we are not aware of. It is our decision if we are more conscious or subconscious, depending on each individual's level of responsibility, or depending on what each person wants in their life.

I am a truth seeker, and I choose consciousness. I practice conscious nutrition; I eat slowly and I savor every bite. There are a lot of people that simply gulp down their food and eat in a subconscious rush which is a big mistake. This is because a high percentage of the vitamins and proteins are lost since chewing properly helps liquify the food. The more liquified the food, the better the nutrient absorption will be processed by the stomach.

This book is not dedicated to nutrition, I actually have a separate book dedicated to that as it really is a topic that I am very passionate about.

Let's carry on with the first layer: the physical body.

In order to become a master of our physical body, I always recommend two kinds of martial arts: TAEKWONDO and KYOKUSHINKAI KARATE. They are two arts that will take us to the extreme of our possibilities and will even allow us to overcome our limits year after year of practice.

I recommend taekwondo because it is an art focusing on the legs; and I recommend Kyokushinkai karate because it is a very disciplined art, based on resistance and coordination.

I'm going to test you; put down the book, stand up, move your left arm in forward circles and your right arm in backward circles at the same time. Depending on your level of coordination, you will either be able to do it without a problem, or you won't, meaning you will most likely laugh because you can't do it.

First, you need to be able to coordinate your physical body before thinking about evolving new neuronal circuits in your functioning mind. When I talk about new neuronal circuits, I'm not referring to one thought, two thoughts, or even three... I'm talking about neuronal circuits, i.e., a huge complex network inside your brain.

If you are not able to control your physical layer, you will not be able to control your mental layer, and your emotional layer even less than that, and of course, the rest of the layers even less than less...

I insist that these two martial arts have been the best investment of my life. The years go by and your fear of everything reduces considerably because you feel stronger and more confident. That produces a psychosomatic effect in the other layers: your mind, heart, energy, and spirit will also feel stronger and more confident both consciously and subconsciously.

Normal people, in their daily life, mainly use their arms to do things, and barely use their legs, except for walking. Let's look at this in more detail. If we observe this from an energetic point of view, when a human being uses his arm, he sends a signal from the brain, through bioelectricity, that travels through the shoulder, elbow, wrist, and finally to the hand to execute the action. I call this "working on low voltage" because the bioelectricity signal has approximately a one-meter distance from head to hand. This is why I strongly recommend Taekwondo - the bioelectricity signal that the brain sends travels through the back, the spinal cord, the leg, the knee, the shin, the ankle, and finally the foot. This bioelectric signal is way more powerful than the previous one, as it could measure up to two meters. I call this "working on high voltage", a concept that for most people will be overlooked.

LOW VOLTAGE (energetic body): head to hand (1 meter)
HIGH VOLTAGE (energetic body): head to foot (approximately 2 meters)

The people that are used to working on a high voltage can overcome trauma in their life better than the people used to working on a low voltage. People who work on a high voltage are able to find more solutions to problems because their brain is a master of working in bioelectrical high voltage.

Both taekwondo and kyokushinkai develop many skills: strength, resistance, speed, readiness, and flexibility etc.

This creates a psychosomatic effect in all of the other layers:
If I have a very flexible body, I will have a flexible mind and heart too.
If I have a strong body, I will have a strong mind and heart too.
If I have a resistant boy, I will have a resistant mind and heart too.
If I have an agile and fast body, I will have a fast and agile mind and heart too.

I must mention that each individual is different, every human being is unique, and therefore there can be exceptions to the rule. For example, I have a friend who is overweight. He is not lazy, just overweight; but he has a very fast and agile mind. Now imagine if he had a body that worked at high voltage…he could triple the strength of his abilities!

Honestly, I have seen this happen. For instance, in my taekwondo classes, I have seen people struggle with stretching and it was hard for them to be flexible. Therefore, when they had to face a problem in their life, they didn't have a flexible mind, and as a result, they ended up yelling, shouting, and not managing the problem properly.
Yelling affects you physically, making your whole body tense, swelling your veins and arteries, and in some cases, breaking some capillaries. If we focus on what happens inside the brain, we have a swollen brain that will later produce migraines.

At this point, it is important to define genetics and epigenetics.
Genetics is what we received from our parents and what we inherited.
Epigenetics is what we do over our life to improve all of our layers; in other words, it would be the path that we have to pursue, to **change**, to improve, and to evolve.
Once we are a master of our physical body, a master of the physical layer, we can begin the journey to be masters of our mental body and the mental layer.

Later in this book, we will dedicate a whole chapter to the brain. However, here we are talking about the mental layer. To emphasize again, the mental layer also has a conscious and a subconscious. For example, if we have a problem and we ask our mind to find some solutions then this action is a totally conscious action because we commanded our mind to start working and thinking. However, we run into issues when our mind works subconsciously, without our consent and we listen to it. For instance, we are doing the dishes and our mind starts thinking without our consent that our partner is flirting with someone else. This is an intrusive thought, and also a subconscious action of our brain. Here´s the problem, if we have the thought and then we listen to it, and believe it… we will have serious complications in our life. Another worrying factor is that our mind started to think without our consent and we didn't even notice! A lot of people, without knowing it, live a subconscious life, enslaved by all of those intrusions, enslaved by all of those intrusive thoughts, and we are here, reading this book, to break free from this mental prison and consequently live a healthier and freer life with less fear. The mind can really become our worst enemy if we are not aware of this information. The key is not to engage with our subconsciousness.

There can be healthy intrusive thoughts and unhealthy intrusive thoughts.
There are two conflicting theories about information in the brain.
1) The information we have is located in the brain, a fact that I find to be false, because the scientific community of the entire world still can´t demonstrate any specific zone or place in the brain that is able to store information.
2) Our brain can be compared to a Wi-Fi antenna, depending on its frequency, it is able to get information from the air, (the collective consciousness), from everyone and everything.

You already know that everything is FREQUENCY (6), ENERGY (3), and VIBRATION (9).
Depending on which frequency we find ourselves during a period of time, our brain, or our
Wi-Fi antenna will be able to connect to other frequencies from the collective consciousness and obtain information in a subconscious manner for us, or in a conscious manner if we are practiced in meditation.
For example, **I have been investigating neuroscience for a long time** (my brain already has been in these frequencies for some time), and one day my cerebral Wi-Fi antenna became activated. I decided to brainstorm my thoughts, so I got a piece of paper and started writing every thought that came to mind. All of this was without my consent, I didn't put my mind to work, it started working by itself. Is that what I wanted? Yes. Is that what I was looking for? Yes. Was it something conscious? No. This is my point, there can be healthy intrusive thoughts. It all depends on our state of frequency, energy, and vibration.
This is the long goal, to detect intrusive thoughts, and discern if they are healthy intrusive thoughts or unhealthy intrusive thoughts; this is a very high level of consciousness. :)

I think that with this introduction to the mental body, we can move on to the emotional body or the emotional layer.
To be honest, whatever I say about this body, I'm going to fall short...
Perhaps you can explain or describe the love that you feel for your children?
No, right? You can't explain that with words, and whatever we say will surely fall short.
Love can't be described with words; words cannot illustrate the complexity of this topic.
That's the reason why this layer is more complicated than the mental one.
With the emotional layer, there is also a conscious and a subconscious part. For example, in life there might be things that you like such as the rubbish collection system in your city; it works efficiently and you feel pride. If things are done properly, it's logical that your heart is activated and it feels good. In fact, you liking it, is something conscious, because it has a logical base.
But there is also a subconscious, this can be something that you like very much but you don't know why. For instance, there are people that enjoy speed, or heights but they don't know why, they just know that they love that adrenaline rush. Or, when you like a girl but you don't know why.

We could say that the physical body, and the mental body, can activate your emotional body. In order for you to like something, there must be some reasoning behind it. Physical, mental or energetic reasons. That's the emotional conscious.

The clearest example of the emotional subconscious is to fall in love with someone that does not love you back. In this case, two things can happen: you keep abusing yourself by not wanting to realize that this person does not love you back, or your emotional intelligence kicks in resulting in an activation of consciousness. I'm talking about your **spirit** becoming activated and this allows you to choose the way for your physical body, then the mental body, and finally the emotional body.
If we have an emotional conflict our spirit can be activated.

In order to verify the social programming and social engineering that we have inside us, I invite you to do the following exercise to activate your arborescent thinking. Unfortunately, we are very much programmed - they have brutally programmed us at school in bad faith. They have activated the subconscious and the fears of all of our layers. The worst thing of all is that they have drilled so many problems into our head with an infinite amount of tasks and chores.

We are so used to thinking with our heads and to feeling with our hearts that we can't see beyond that...

Put down the book for a few minutes to do the following deprogramming exercise. Whilst reading it, you should actually try to do it and feel it in your being. Focus on these words:

THINK WITH YOUR HEART, FEEL WITH YOUR HEAD
THINK WITH YOUR HEART, FEEL WITH YOUR HEAD
THINK WITH YOUR HEART, FEEL WITH YOUR HEAD

If you have managed to do it, you have understood the level of programming within us, and also you have realized that we can deprogram and reprogram ourselves. Not everything they told us is true, it's most likely the contrary...everything they told us is a lie. I hope you start having notions of **the arborescent way of thinking and the infinite possibilities.**

Let's dive deeper into the magnetic body. I know you may have heard of Traditional Chinese Medicine (TCM). TCM is connected to the energetic body though Tai Chi and its grandfather, Chi kung – Qigong. I also know that you may have heard about acupuncture and the energetic meridians, through which our energy flow circulates, our Qi.

Let's do a simple exercise, put the book down and close it. Once you have done that, stand in front of a mirror, (or even without a mirror – it doesn´t matter), and put on a very serious face and hold it for a few seconds. After those seconds, relax and give yourself a smile - you will feel how your energetic body has activated.
I'm sure that in the past whenever you saw a girl or a boy that you liked, your energetic body became activated. Honestly, this is one of the most beautiful things in life - the fact that you like another being physically, mentally, emotionally, but also energetically. To feel the attraction with all of the layers - this

has only happened to me three times in my life. The last time that it happened was the most powerful because I totally felt that she was my soulmate, and to be honest, I still feel like this. However, for one or another reason, it was not meant to be.

Of course, energy has a conscious and a subconscious too. The energetic layer can be activated without our consent, or it can be activated by us, such as with the exercises I outlined before with the serious and smiling face or through Chi Kung – Qigong. We also activated our energetic body when we did the exercise dedicated to thinking with our heart and feeling with our head - breaking our programming. Every time we deprogram ourselves from something, there is a *protein rain* in our brains produced by this energetic body. Every time we reprogram ourselves with new neuronal circuits through exercises, we produce protein explosions in our brain's neurons.

Doing the "think with your heart – feel with your head" exercise may have been your first experience with deprogramming and reprogramming. It may have been the first time you installed new neuronal circuits in your brain. This complex kind of process is called "working our microcosm" or "inner work".

Sometimes the energetic body is also activated when you make eye contact with let´s say, a blonde girl on the street, or with a brunette waiting for the traffic lights. This situation can be either stem from healthy or unhealthy energies. From now on, pay more attention to your energetic body.

In my opinion, the energetic layer is the most crucial aspect because sometimes people don't know how to do something, or how to say something, and they can throw you some energetic punches that hurt and remain for some time. People should be much more responsible about their way of doing and saying things.

TO ME, THE MOST IMPORTANT LAYER IS ONE THAT NOBODY SEES: THE ENERGETIC BODY.

For those of us who have really developed the energetic body, if we are with some friends and another friend joins the group, we can sense how this person is feeling, without even looking at them. If they feel good, we will sense a lighter atmosphere; if they feel bad, we will sense very dense and heavy energies in the room.

Of course, to develop the energetic body, you need to build your physical body, followed by the mental body, and lastly, we must develop the emotional body. When you can adequately manage these three bodies, in both their subconscious and conscious forms... we could say that you start to walk on a different path; you start being supernatural.
In addition to this, it´s important to mention that each of us has a toroidal energetic field *(from now on referred to as a "toroid field")*, but there is also a collective energy created from all of us. For example, a group of friends will have a toroid field, neighbors will have another toroid field, a whole town will have an even bigger toroid field, and the entire world we have another toroid field.

This energy is simply all around, you feel it and you sense it. Depending on our mood we can either ignore it, or nourish it. This is why we should all be more responsible with what happens inside our body, because if I have negative feelings, it's going to affect everyone, whether we like it or not, it will affect the collective energy. The same goes with our mind, our heart and our collective consciousness. So please, start taking this very seriously, because if some people are feeling bad, it is affecting everyone, whether we like it or not, this is what happens. That's why we often say that "we all are at one." Even if I'm conscious that some people will never change, I still have some doubts about if there are some *clones* amongst the population, people that do not feel nor suffer... Surely you have thought about this too, that many things that you experience are not adding up... Many things that people do, you don't consider those actions or words as really human.
I'm sure that you have encountered these people that do not feel nor suffer, and you thought to yourself - "Seriously, how could you be like this?".

When we think about *clones* amongst the population it is something truly serious that will activate the arborescent thinking and infinite possibilities of your mind.
Pay attention, and try to identify people who are more human and sensitive.

I must insist that the energetic layer is the most essential part of a human being. All of our lost energetic life is based on drainages, in other words, specific circumstances that drain us.

You must try to develop the energetic layer, because depending on the actions of others, you can receive energetic punches. Moreover, you can also give these punches. These energetic punches can be conscious, or subconscious. Conscious punches: This is when you purposely try to hurt someone and it can be done in many ways, for example, if you try to make your partner jealous. You can upload a profile picture of you and a friend of the opposite sex, and this can result in an energetic punch for your partner. Sometimes bad things can happen in relationships, and people may feel the need for revenge. They end up getting revenge one way or another; without being conscious of their energetic body, and severe energetic damage is done. Other times, due to lack of awareness, being *clones* or pure ignorance, energetic punches can be thrown subconsciously, without thinking it or feeling it.

The more conscious human beings are of this fact, the healthier human relationships will be, and this is very important for the "drainage" factor. We should ask: -"Do you realize that we are draining ourselves?" "Do you realize that you are draining me?"-

Later in this book, we will talk about other beings in other planes that feed on these potential differences; in other words, there are beings that feed on our energetic voltages. This is the foundation of this book, to realize that we suffer from energetic losses in our life through our different layers. We can have energetic losses in our physical body, and also we can suffer energetic losses through our brain, due to some mental shock that we can't understand, and then we wonder "Why is this happening to me?"

In addition, we can have emotional shocks, and suffer drainages from the emotional body in our heart. I know that you remember and relive some harsh situations or shocks that you may have experienced in the past, but don't worry, we are here to **heal** everything.

I have my own theory about life and death with regards to collective energy; let me explain. We are individuals; therefore, we are here to live in individuality. So, when we die, we are the opposite of individuality; we are the totality and become part of the whole. I think that people who die, don't actually die, but in fact they become part of collective energy. For example, my grandfather who passed away some years ago, is in every drop of my being, in every drop of your being, in every hair of my eyebrow, or in every hair of your head, in every thought… I'm talking about in an energetic way, he is there.

Therefore, people should celebrate every demise instead of concentrating so much on satanism…where the whole family cries, multiple drainages and complete discomfort. This does not nourish us; instead, it intoxicates us, and creates mental, emotional and energetic shocks, vibrating out into death's energy frequency.

I understand that everything in life is connected to cycles, and when we bury a person in a coffin, or cremate them and scatter the ashes at sea, the life cycle is broken. Deceased bodies should be decomposed by worms and soil, in order to be part of the whole. I don't understand the fascination of keeping the ashes of a loved one in the house, breaking the energetic cycle, encouraging the act of attachment, and not wanting them to leave. They have already left. People who don't want to see are blind. Neither do I understand the people who chose to be inside the coffin, breaking the energetic cycle.

So I hope that the layers of the body are becoming clearer:

 - Physical layer – (physical plane) *body – physical body (1)*
 - Mental layer – (mental plane) *soul – etheric body (2)*
 - Emotional layer – (emotional plane) *soul – etheric body (2)*
 - Energetic layer – (energetic plane) *soul – etheric body (2)*
 - Spiritual layer – (spiritual plane) *spirit – light body (3)*

The spirit is the force that we have within that can make us feel extremely powerful and eternal. The spirit has everything, it is complete, and does not need anything or anyone.

A way to recognize your spiritual body is to be a master in recognition.

For example, do the following exercise:
Put down the book, and take a few seconds or minutes for yourself. You must forget about your body, about your mind, about your heart and about your energy. Investigate and delve deep within yourself, at your solar plexus level, in your chest. If you do find something, if you recognize yourself…that inner force, is the same inner force that I also have inside of *my* chest. That's why we must respect each other. We really are one, we are all made up of the same ´one´, we are all reflections of each other. In this aspect, you are me and I am you. **The spirit has a certain character and certain power, it is the light body.** This ability to recognize yourself for real, the clones won't be able to do it. Moreover, they will probably ridicule and ignore this information, because that's how clones are, they don't care about anything, except to show indifference; just living their physical lives and displaying their ego is enough for them. They most certainly prefer to talk about football or such things, or to get drunk over a few beers than talk about these very important topics.

Hence, we need to have something very clear, *"Do not give what is holy to the dogs; nor cast your pearls before a swine"* states the famous quote - and the sooner you notice that not all of us are human beings, the earlier you will start to love yourself more and appreciate yourself. I wasted so much time with these clones, and the worst thing of all is that they end up draining you. Sometimes you come home, exhausted, wondering – "Why did I go out today? I feel like they sucked out all of my energy"-.
Maybe you are not really conscious of what you are, energetically speaking, of how they drain you. Neither are you conscious of which beings you spend your time with.
I really know some people with a naked spirit, people that have liberated themselves from their burdens almost completely. People that detect and spot their mental scourge and stigma, people that detect their emotional scourge, and people that detect their physical scourge. They live in peace with themselves and with others. They are really admirable people who are liberated and already walk on the supernatural path.

This is really what we seek, peace and tranquility because at the moment that this is broken, and we suffer wars internally or externally, then is when we are being drained. Not only are we not living in the present, but we are not appreciating ourselves, and therefore we can end up ceasing to love ourselves. Consequently, when the head, the heart and our energies start misfunctioning… we can fall into self-sabotage, and into abusing our mind, heart, and energy.

However, that's what this book is for, to spot these things and love ourselves again.
In order to become masters of these five bodies, first we must know how to differentiate them, how to identify them, and detect when they get activated. Once we can do that, we can dominate these practices.

I really believe that this is one of the biggest secrets of life they hide from us, because you didn't come to this life to work as a slave and to be fooled like a fool.
Notice how well they have set this up, how there is absolute social programming. Social engineering

programs the physical body massively. It makes our physical body activate at high levels, forgetting about the rest of our bodies. For example, with our eyes: look at your neighbor's car, look at your uncle's house, look at the legs that appear on TV, look at those clothes. These are desires and hyper-sexualization. We suffer a constant disproportionate sexual bombing everywhere, either because people dress up revealing much more than they should, or because it appears on TV or on the radio, even through music. The whole world listens to reggaeton, and this is something I can't understand. **If you take away the music and the rhythm in reggaeton, the result is a man harassing you.**

The people that rule the world know this, that's why they created the social engineering or social programming in which I can see a lot of victims in this Matrix, made by them to distract you so you can't see or you don't pay attention to the rest of the bodies that you have. Furthermore, they know about conscious programming techniques and subconscious programming techniques as well, and this is dangerous. It's clear that a little girl that listens to reggaeton her whole life, even without wanting to, without being conscious of it and without her consent, as a product, she will be a troubled woman. The same happens with men too: slaves of luxuries, slaves of posing (acting fake to look cool), slaves of hyper-sexualization.

**All of this is focused on keeping them stuck in the first body, so they can't see further.
Like this, you will have docile and compliant people, manipulable, slave-like, and shortsighted.
NOT VERY HUMAN PEOPLE.**

We will revise the whole brain in depth, but also that the social engineering or social programming has wreaked havoc in the brain because they completely activated the left hemisphere of the brain. They know this, and they want us to be square-headed, like that chair, like that table, like that blackboard in the classroom, like that squared-head teacher... Not to mention worldwide fluoridation; fluoride is the most stupidity-inducing element from the periodic table, besides being the first cause of cavities. As we are on this topic, we could also talk about geoengineering (making it hard to see bright blue skies or pompous 3D clouds nowadays), or about the H.A.A.R.P. project, with which they radiate us almost every day. You just have to go out to the street, look at the sky, and focus on those clouds with a wavy shape. They are waves that comply with electromagnetic frequency patterns.

The sabotages that our brain suffers are constant, and the more we know about it, the stronger we will be, because information is power.

In addition, we haven't even mentioned the poisons in meat, with hormones; plastic food and transgenic food. They really make a big effort so that we don't evolve. The ones who rule the world are interested in having us muddle-headed and numb, and if we are **distracted,** suffering drainages, even better. That's why drugs exist, some of them even legalized under the forms of alcohol and tobacco.

**It seems that love and emotions are old-fashioned concepts in this system, and they are completely pushed into the background. (Everything is aimed at the physical body and to brainwash us).
Just the fact that the energetic body and the spirit aren´t even mentioned by the system proves my point... we don't even know it exists.**

I will leave this blank page if you want to write any insights, learnings, or anything else that caught your attention:

2: THE HUMAN BRAIN

The people who say you don't need to control your physical body in order to control your mind, are totally wrong. The clearest example of this is when sitting at a table, you accidentally knock over, I repeat, *accidentally*, a glass of water, and soak another person. This person usually jumps up enraged, or at least shouts at you "What are you doing?!" ... Really, spilling some water on another human being, I believe, is not a crime, and they are draining your energy if they yell at you.

At the very moment that we see a glass of water spilling over a part of our body, a lot of neuronal circuits start working, altering our consciousness. To this, we add the automatic responses of the physical body expressing to you the concept "wetness". During this complex system of information that occurs in less than two seconds, we find two kinds of results: people who can control themselves, and are conscious that nothing wrong really happened; and the people who cannot, and they yell. In other words, people who are not energetically drained and those who are energetically drained. People with high levels of intelligence will laugh at the situation since it wasn't a serious problem at all.

My point is that there are many people who do not actually live their life, but they are living a subconscious life, **enslaved by the automatisms of their body, enslaved by their mind and offended little heart.** They live what their head and body dictate them, without being conscious that they can transmute and transform reality. They are unaware that they can start taking control of their present life.

For instance, for people who practice martial arts, and can take physical hits in a fight, it is more than clear that this fact produces a psychosomatic effect in the mind, and thus the mind expands so they will mentally be able to take certain hits without fear or trembling.
When we also factor in the information in this book, our abilities will be enhanced.

Let's start with the parts of the brain. First, let's see the hemispheres; left and right.

The left hemisphere, that is the one that they activate the most, is called the **convergent brain** and in it we can find the following words: logic, analysis, reasoning, numerology, practice, strategy, **control**, science, verbal, rational, quantitative, deductive, **simplify**, specialize, **separate**, critic, objective-orientated, sequential, literal, <u>rule-abider</u>, systemic, etc.

The right hemisphere, which we have almost deactivated, is called the **divergent brain** and in it we can find the following words: intuition, **passion**, freedom, union, creativity, **peace**, visual, qualitative, synthesize, inductive, enrich, integrate, connect, non-judging, wholeness-oriented, simultaneous, subjective, metaphoric, not worried about rules, directed towards the process, empathic, etc.

One of the absolute truths is that we are not natural human beings, but actually a product of a disloyal system. **We are a product of manipulation** in all senses, from the moment we are born until we die. It is up to us to take control of our own life and deprogram ourselves from any mental, physical and emotional chatter and noise. It is time to hack our being, it is time to hack our microcosm and become more human than ever.

A new and more humane world can only be reached if its people are *newer* and more humane. For this reason, we need to dispose of what has been learned, expand our minds, and understand our microcosm.

Now, let's look at the different types of brain, from the outer to the inner: the rational brain, the emotional brain, and the instinctive brain. Also known as: the neocortex, the limbic and the reptilian or primal.

THE NEOCORTEX: is the base of consciousness. This brain is addicted to receiving information, listening, living in the present at its fullest, to paying attention. In fact, you are using it right now to read my words and my sentences so expectantly. Depending of the type of thought, it will be processed in the lateral part, frontal part, the upper part or on the rear part of the neocortex. I recommend that you google these images: the three brains.

I love the neocortex because it is the base of the learning process, it is with the neocortex that we listen. Also, if we have any type of problem, and we put our head to work in a conscious way, it is the neocortex that will find the solution. It is the most external part of our brain.

THE LIMBIC BRAIN: animals don't have a neocortex; their brain expands to just the limbic brain. I'm not saying that they can't learn or listen, but they do in their own way. I believe that animals are more evolved than the human being, simply because they have more empathy most of the time. Whereas a human being is capable to put himself above anything else, especially the unconscious human being. Meanwhile, if you are reading this book, you analyze it properly and integrate it deeper into your mind, you are already using the limbic brain. In fact, if in the following days you realize certain things learned in this book and you apply them, you are activating your microcosm; that is, using the limbic brain. Here is an example: if I tell you a chickpea hummus recipe, reading it or listening to it is done with the neocortex. However, if you actually carry out the recipe, and prepare the hummus, that would be activating the limbic brain, and here lies the secret of long-term memory. If you use the limbic brain several times with a certain activity, it is certain that your long-term memory will get activated effectively. I call this, eternal memorization. It's a pity that they don't teach you this in school, but of course, they want you to be fooled.

People who practice martial arts have the limbic brain more developed, because when the master explains, we pay attention and listen with our neocortex; but after a short space of time, the master tells you to perform the exercises whilst activating the limbic brain. In other words, he doesn't force you to pass the information from the neocortex to the limbic brain, but it happens naturally every day that we go to class.

The limbic brain is also known as the emotional brain, it is here where several neuronal circuits start working when we feel something. Here the emotion is detected or provoked.

THE REPTILIAN (OR PRIMAL) BRAIN: is the inner part of the brain. It has this name because some animals only have this type of brain and they are genuine predators, like the Gaboon Viper. The reptilian brain houses our subconscious; this is the culprit of most impulses we have, such as human disputes. If this brain takes control, we become slaves and operate subconsciously. It is connected to the spinal cord and the cerebellum, here is where the concepts of "perpetuate the species" and "extreme survival" lie. It has its good points, but also some bad ones. In martial arts, practicing for so many days, and for many years, if someone attacks us, our defense or our blocking or our response or our anticipation will be executed instantly and subconsciously. This is because we have everything well-integrated already, like second nature.

I'm going to challenge you, so you can see that you don't have it tamed. **Close the book,** and walk around your house. If you are able to walk in peace and silence, you get a positive point. If instead you walk around your house and a multitude of thoughts come to your mind, you will realize all of the subconscious thoughts that you listen to. You will realize your mental scourge and all of the noise we have inside of us. I remind you, that this was a simple exercise, just walking around your house in silence, but a silence both internal and external is hard to achieve.

I think you will now understand the big problem that we face with our intrusive thoughts.

Many times, I have been in the kitchen doing the dishes, and I have noticed the mental chatter I have inside my mind. **The key is simply practicing concentration, conscious breathing and knowing how to vibrate inside of oneself, but it's important to know how to vibrate inside of oneself in lucid states at the present time, not vibrating in the past and not vibrating in the future** (meaning, to set our vibration from within, not the other way; not to set the vibration to the past, neither to the future; but in the present time). If we vibrate in the past, we will vibrate in melancholy and sorrow, and we can generate a lung disease because sadness is the emotion that can attack the lungs. If we vibrate in the future, we will vibrate in anxiety, and we can generate heart disease, because anxiety is the emotion that attacks the heart.

This sentence is the most important one of the book, **know how to vibrate within, inside of yourself, but mainly you should know how to vibrate within yourself in lucid states IN THE PRESENT, not in the past nor in the future.** That is the key to living and appreciating the present in all its possible ways, that is the key to being free and protecting ourselves from intrusive thoughts.

The worst part of not knowing this, is that you could be in the kitchen doing the dishes, with that mental noise, and start listening to your mind, which just started working without your consent. Well, once you start paying attention to your mind, your mind acquires the main role, and you can end up believing 100% what it is telling you, even if it's true or a lie.

A friend of mine (Sara), had this situation while doing the dishes... Her mind, WITHOUT HER CONSENT, all of the sudden started thinking that her boyfriend could be with another girl (1st intrusive thought). Then, she started thinking: which girl could it be? (2nd intrusive thought). After that, her mind told her that surely her boyfriend was with a girl named Veronica (3rd intrusive thought). Thereafter, her mind reminded her where that Veronica girl lives, and therefore she visualized her house and her neighborhood (4th intrusive thought).

My friend Sara started feeling really anxious, and it was all subconscious; she wasn't conscious about it until I explained it to her. Do you know how this story goes on? Sara had so many intrusive thoughts, so many subconscious thoughts. She was living her subconscious life being a slave of her mind without even noticing it. Her mind kept working, dynamiting her life; she took the car keys, left the house, got into the car, and started looking for her boyfriend and Veronica around the neighborhood. More and more anguished she became, speeding up with her car, like a crazy girl, possessed and parasitized. SARA STOPPED BEING SARA at the moment when that 1st intrusive thought sneaked into her mind. She almost crashed the car; she felt like killing her boyfriend and Veronica, look how far intrusive thoughts can go. My friend Sara, called her boyfriend yelling at him in a disrespectful tone: - 'Where are you, you wretched little man?!'

Her boyfriend was at home, having dinner with his parents because it was his father's birthday and Sara had just forgotten about that...

Notice the extent to which the mind can sabotage us, that we stop what we were doing, we stop living our present and in fact, due to our lack of mastery of our microcosm, our mind takes over control of our life, forcing us to live an anguished lie.

Now we have to be clear about one thing, you are using the neocortex to know all of this; it's in your hand to bring that information to the limbic brain and practice all of this as a master of your microcosm. That´s the time to detect the subconscious intrusive thoughts.

If you want to be an empowered human being, it's your decision. Now you have this knowledge and I hope that you apply it and wake up for real. Even if you still have a long way to go, I promise that now your new conscious life begins, but the decision is yours.

I must underline that the problem is always that your mind starts thinking without your consent, by itself. Once activated, the problem is if we listen to it, and even worse, if we believe it. Here is where all problems start and here is where you are enslaved by your mind living a subconscious life.
It is then when your mind is making the decisions, not you, and not consciously.

As far as I am concerned, I am an empowered being, I decide what goes into my being and what doesn't. It is true that I have lived through many shocking things, and I have delved into this a lot in order to become a master of my consciousness and mainly to be able to explain this great complexity that lies within us.

I must acknowledge that sometimes I see people I´m close with, acting subconsciously, and it really hurts me, because they are not conscious of the harm they are causing me, subconsciously. It is also true that I have explained this to them, and I have talked about it. I have even made some videos explaining all of this, but many times I have seen subconscious behaviors that are too much for me and **I ended up**

giving up on a lot of people. The problem that we, the very conscious people, have; is that the level is very high and it increases more and more, so we are highly 'demanding', especially because we don't allow people to mistreat us. This is one of the most important things in life for me: DO NOT MISTREAT ME. Of course, if I apply this to me, I apply it to other people; I do not mistreat or abuse anybody - physically, mentally, verbally, emotionally, energetically or spiritually. I have never harassed anybody.

Now you are going to know something about me; I want to tell you about the first time I discovered my subconscious, the first time that I caught my mind thinking without my consent. If you train this, you can achieve a positive mastery of yourself, be able to live without intrusions, and be able to live a freer life by making conscious decisions.

Where I live, there is a gardener that does as best as he can. Let's say that he is quite smart but not a brainiac, but it's not our job to judge him. Most of the neighbors there hate him; my father, for instance, every time he sees the gardener, says: 'Fucking shit gardener'...
That hate, ended up impregnating my subconscious without me noticing it (exactly as it happens when the TV is on and we are doing things in the house, without paying much attention - be careful with this). As the years went by, I started feeling disgusted by the gardener, and started to rant about him in my mind every time I saw him. This information came to me thanks to JOE DISPENZA. I was going home and I saw the gardener, my mind started thinking negative thoughts about him without my consent, until I finally realized. What was happening inside of me? Where did all that hate come from? If he never did anything wrong to me. That was when I realized, that my mind was thinking by itself, automatically, and I was listening to it and was even believing those thoughts. I had detected my subconscious for the first time, so I expectantly observed how all this programming and automatisms were behaving inside of me. After a while, I laughed, and I told my mind: Hey, mind! This is the last time that you shake things up by screwing with my present. I must confess, that I had caught it a bit late, it was already on the fifth intrusive thought or so. I had already done the first step, now I had to specialize in catching my mind earlier, like on the fourth intrusive thought, or on the third one...to detect it as soon as possible.

That's why I'm telling you, that this is a mastery, where you can specialize in and become great on the inside. The years passed by, and when intrusive thoughts come to my mind, now I'm able to spot them at the first sign and I don't even let the first toxic intrusive thought develop. The problem is, and you will see this further on, that sometimes the trigger of those intrusive thoughts is actually not the mind, but other aspects that produce them; like intrusive feelings or intrusive energies.

The truth is, the people who don't have this knowledge, really abuse themselves and abuse others, and it hurts me a lot to see this behavior of the human being. I guess I could be an old spirit of this world, that came here to activate others' spirits - like nobody has even done before to humanity. I remind you that this old spirit that I have within me, is the same one that you have within yourself :)

Up until now, I haven't let anything contaminate 'my royalty', and sometimes I think that some external dark force, uses weak people or clones to sabotage my present time from the macrocosm, **because**

there is no more inner toxicity from me, towards me. It is true, that the more you know, the more responsibility you have, the bigger the effort required and the fiercer the battle. If you follow this path of consciousness, you will realize; that maybe you will receive more attacks from outer forces.

I wanted to emphasize something: when I caught my mind producing toxic thoughts about the gardener, I told it "Stop doing that", meaning that I deprogrammed it, I noticed it, and I was conscious about it. JOE DISPENZA tells us that when you deactivate old neuronal circuits and when you activate new neuronal circuits, protein explosions are produced in our brain. This could be a new nutrition method for the human being, in order to not overwork our genes. For instance, if you wear down the same gene, it ages your brain, and ages your body. Some people wake up, carry out the same routine, look at themselves in the bathroom mirror, grab their favorite mug… That activates premature aging due to genetic abuse, by using the same genes every day. To go further, I invite you to have your breakfast in a pot, or in a different cup, or don't have breakfast at all, or that when you have it, have it in a different spot every day: have breakfast in the bathroom, in the bedroom, on the balcony, in the garden… have breakfast in all the different places of your home. This will deactivate old neuronal circuits and will activate new neuronal circuits; which could make you laugh. For example, sometimes I walk down the stairs sideways, or backwards (but carefully). Start doing new things in your life, to activate new neuronal circuits. Routines and habits wear our mind's genes out and make us age.

To be a magician within us is a mastery, you must try to achieve the black belt.

Let me continue; the next day I saw the gardener, I noticed my mind wanting to think without my consent and I stopped it, I closed the door even before the first intrusive thought reached 5%. I passed the gardener and told him: ´Hello! Have a nice day!´
By doing this, and changing my macrocosm, I was using the limbic brain, moving from theory to practice, moving from being a pupil to being a master for the first time. By doing this, we are entering into epigenetics. In other words, we start to develop our energetic path, because activating new neuronal circuits is about epigenetics.
Here is when our inner magician, our spirit, is empowered, is recognized, and commands over and above the body, mind, and heart. Effectively I had changed my present and his present, in a positive way, or at least in a healthier way. This was quite different from before, with all of those dirty looks and intrusive thoughts. From then on, your consciousness is activated. The next time I heard someone criticizing the gardener, I defended him, and slowly all of the neighbors stopped hating him except for the typical clone that kept hating him, hating me, and hating the entire neighborhood.

I want to tell you that you can really be the owner of your life, you can own your present and you can be the owner of how your life develops in this plane.
We are made up of 30 billion cells, we should be more responsible with our microcosm, we should be more responsible with "the city and the citizens" that we have within us.

I want you to focus on that from an energetic point of view, 30 billion cells! That is pure vibration, imagine if they all vibrated in the energy of joy, in the spirit's frequency at high vibrations. It would be an energetic portal of pure light in the astral plane and of pure bioelectricity in the energetic body.

Sure, if you have intrusive thoughts, and you don't spot them, and you let your microcosm be contaminated, actually it is 30 billion cells vibrating in contaminant energy at low frequencies. This will affect the collective energy as I said before.

Would you hurt me? Would you like to make me feel bad even minimally? (I guess the answer is "no".) Then become an empowered human being and be careful that your energies do not contaminate the collective energy, so the collective energy does not contaminate me. We are in a difficult era, regarding collective energy, since we have the whole planet full of intrusive thoughts due to the fear provoked by TV and other media sources. I encourage you to google the meaning of "state terrorism". They have always been interested in having us between *fear* and *terror*, distracted, so we don't evolve. Why do you think it is called ´corona´? Simply because your corona chakra, is the highest chakra of your being, and if it's decreased, it prevents your consciousness from expanding.

If you really want to hurt me, it is not you, it is your subconscious, your egos, or some parasitism; because the human being is good by nature, and is brilliant.

As well as a collective consciousness, there is also a collective subconsciousness. In the collective subconscious, we find the archetypes. I'm sure that you have seen that video about four babies hugging each other many times and laughing. Knowing how to hug is an archetype. Nobody taught the babies how to do that, it's a "by default" human skill.

Let's do another exercise; close the book and explain to yourself everything we learned so far. Don't forget about the three brains, their hemispheres and about the archetypes.

DON'T GET OFFENDED
FREE YOURSELF FROM THE NEED TO WIN
FREE YOURSELF FROM THE NEED TO BE RIGHT
FREE YOURSELF FROM THE NEED OF BEING SUPERIOR TO OTHERS
FREE YOURSELF FROM THE NEED OF FAME
FREE YOURSELF OF THE NEED OF MEANINGLESSLY HAVING MORE (pointless greed)

I would like to tell you, after all of that, don't be afraid to eliminate toxic people from your life, the ones that don't nourish you or don't add to your wellness. Moreover, get away from people that drain your energy. Likewise, stop watching things that don't nourish you and don't contribute anything positive, a good example would be the TV. If you spend time with those toxicities, if you "water" toxic people or toxic things, that is how the world will be, a toxic world. **It is very important that we stop nurturing toxic things and turn our backs on them.** When you start walking the NON-TOXIC path, really powerful beings will enter your life, and they will be as nurturing as you or even more. There won't be many, but you will find them, I promise. If you don't cut your toxic bonds with other toxic people or things... they will be draining and distracting you from what is really important, like living in the present, at ease and peacefully, without being coerced.

I DIDN'T COME TO LIVE A FEARFUL LIFE
WHEN YOU CLOSE A BLACK DOOR IN YOUR LIFE
THREE WHITE WINDOWS OPEN IN FRONT OF YOU

Honestly, I have cut out many people from my old life in the last few years. The fact that half of our population is still kind of ´prehistoric´, is pretty shameful, as if we have gone backwards in time instead of evolving. That's why insist on always being aware of our conscious and of your subconscious.

*I am going to propose another exercise (do it as many times as you want). It is about toxicity in your life.

Write 3 good things that happened today:

Write 3 bad things that happened today:

Now in each case, measure roughly the percentage % of your own involvement that may have caused those situations.

I have now offered a lot of information about convergent and divergent hemispheres, about the three brains; (neocortex, limbic and reptilian), and about the archetypes. Now, I think it's time to talk about the famous NEGATIVE PRIMING.

This concept consists of totally subconscious programming. In a large number of movies or TV shows they tell us a big hidden truth, and immediately we can hear the audience laughing. Due to repeatedly programming the brain with this emotional impulse of truth-laughter, your brain gets programmed so when you really hear a big "hidden" truth, you will automatically laugh. There are many good videos on the internet about negative priming.

It's a way of shaping the perfect *sheeple* that will never question anything.

In order to fully understand this, we have to focus on the two kinds of memory: declarative memory and procedural memory.

DECLARATIVE MEMORY: (part of explicit memories)
- **Episodic memory:** allows us to recover specific experiences
- **Semantic memory:** lexicon knowledge, concepts and categories (facts)

Both allow you to recover the information VOLUNTARILY

PROCEDURAL MEMORY:
- **Implicit memory:** long-term memory that doesn't require voluntariness, its effects are maintained over time. **In the implicit memory, we have negative priming.**
- **Conditioning:** if, for example, we are training a taekwondo kick, and we make any kind of mistake while executing it, the error stimulus will be perfected by the error. If, otherwise, we perform a perfect and neat kick, the accuracy will be perfected.
- **Motor skills:** they refer to conditioning. We can have motor skills towards the error or towards success and accuracy.

Emotional memory does not allow us to recall the elements that created it. It produces a feeling of rejection or a feeling of total acceptance.

Social programming or social engineering is based on this.

COGNITIVE DISSONANCE:

Sometimes, some people hold a very strong fundamental core belief. When you present evidence that goes against their belief, **the new evidence can't be accepted. AN UNCOMFORTABLE SENSATION CALLED COGNITIVE DISSONANCE IS CREATED.** Due to the importance of protecting that fundamental belief, anything that doesn't fit with that core belief will be rationalized, ignored or even denied.

All of this is generated by the so-called **belief systems.**

After all, beliefs are simply that, just beliefs. They could no longer be beliefs if they really checked them. However, people live deep in the social programming of a commodity. For instance, something as beautiful as educating and homeschooling our children is not done anymore, or it happens rarely. We let other people educate and teach them at school. This great and marvelous responsibility is left to others. On top of that, parents will get angry if their children are rebellious. In fact, human beings are being completely dehumanized. They are rebellious due to a lack of affection from their parents. I can understand, and can see it as normal - think about being in class, with complete strangers as teachers. These teachers, in some cases, will ignore students even more than their parents do, or even will expel you from class - this used to happen to me. Or in other cases, some teachers will pick their favorite students; not to mention that girls always got better grades than me, even when they had copied my exam, or sometimes even worse things...

The key to negative priming, is to introduce in a human being's mind, through the TV, a truth followed by laughter, so when we really find the truth, it will be difficult to assimilate that truth or to the point, that we even end up explicitly rejecting it. Watch out next time when someone tells you something shocking, will you reject it and laugh about it, or will you be humbler by having empathy towards who's telling you the story by activating arborescent thinking?

Negative PRIMING is known in psychology for being a defect related to implicit memory, so consequently, the explosion to certain stimulus has influence over the response of stimulus submitted subsequently. In other words, all the information that the brain gathers, WILL DETERMINE THE WAY OF ACTING OR MAKING DECISIONS IN THE FUTURE IN AN UNCONSCIOUS MANNER.
We must be clear about the brain's glands, their names, and their function. We have the pituitary gland which is a transmitter, good for telepathy emission for example. And the pineal gland, which is a receiver, is good for clairvoyance. Further on we will talk about how to control those glands and how to train them. The intrusions are made through the pineal gland; through it, we can certainly be parasitized from other planes.

I will leave this blank page for you, if you want to write any insights, learnings or anything else that caught your attention:

3 THE ETHERIC CONTRACS

I am aware that we are talking about the human brain, but it really is our best tool to discover certain things such as activating and carrying out the inner study of our body or our microcosm. This is how we deprogram and reprogram ourselves.

We talked about some brain deprogramming, like the case of the gardener being hated by everybody. But there is something else, something on an emotional level in which we must also focus, operate, program, and deprogram. It is our emotional impulse.

First of all, we need willingness to change, otherwise, no kind of evolution will happen. You need to be willing to change, and a lot of people lack this willingness, or don't dare to change.

Secondly, it´s necessary to have the need to realize the reality we live in, and this is a shock. It's necessary to get rid of all kinds of angel invocations, light beings, etc. We must be careful with etheric contracts. Whether it is a little Jesus, a little Yahweh or a superior being with powers...we need to cut off all that, this type of witchcraft is quite dangerous, it is social programming. I was a victim of this too, and I asked for things. Many times nothing even happened, like there was nobody listening, and other times my requests were granted, but it always came with a (negative) little present, a rather hard failure.

The third point is to be comfortable with yourself, to know how to be at ease, to be at peace. To get rid of the need of asking anyone for anything. This will be done by cutting off those etheric contracts. Your will needs to be present. I can't work inside of you, this is up to you and your will.

The fourth point is an observation process, how do you act when you are alone, and how do you act when in front of other people? **How much do you hurt people when you speak to them?** Here is where the EMOTIONAL IMPULSE comes in, the impulse that you may provoke or that others may provoke in you.

The fifth point is to start bringing light to that dark zone we all have, these internal energies of ours that we must work on. You are lacking speed in realizing this, here is where we must work the most. You must realize this, but the truth is a difficult pill to swallow. It's like the hunter and the prey, you are not going to kill it, but to bring it to light, and with time this EMOTIONAL IMPULSE will weaken and lose strength. With time, these things that happened to you in a terrible way most surely will make you laugh, and you will think. ´But how could I be so silly?´ –

Later, you will notice, that there are some beings existing in other planes that feed on all those energetic shocks. These larvae, these parasites, you must learn to stop feeding them.

It is true that we must be careful with our parents' teachings. For example, your father always tells you that you are not enough and that you are miserable. In the end, it seems he's right because that is how you are feeling. It is your responsibility to deprogram yourself, no one else is going to make it but you. It could be also that you come from a very religious family, always praying; and sure, that's hard, because it was your mother or father who taught you this. Even they were mistaken, it's hard, it's a shock.

Similarly, there is a fear or lack of responsibility about taking care of oneself. It´s better to pray, to give your energy to the outer beings, make etheric contracts and generate etheric cords, it can even generate etheric implants. Above all, I will insist that we are the true gods within us. That's why it is so important to vibrate inside of us in states of lucidity, not vibrating in the past nor in the future, and of course, not vibrating outside of us which just gives our energy away.

Like in all contracts, there is the fine print. This is so we don't see it, there is always something hidden that is meant to not be shown, otherwise it would be too visible and result in not signing the contract. The same happens with etheric contracts.

An etheric contract is a belief of something higher out there, a prayer, a request for help, a relief…I need money, I need a partner… from a supposed angel, a supposed god…
THE REQUEST ACTIVATES THE CONTRACT.
The need to ask means there is something missing.
You feel like a 'lacking' being, a poor being, with low self-esteem, and the environment was responsible for this. It left you submissive, lacking, needy and then you request…this is where the contract appears. You are working with low energy, and on top of that, you are vibrating outside of yourself.
If you make a very intense request, the contract will have the same intensity; beware. Many people were into religions without believing too much in the trap, and they made weak contracts and requests.

They can be more carnal requests or more minor carnal requests.
Depending on many things, they can deliver your request, but be ready because it will come with issues, and you will probably suffer something sub-realist (surrealist) in your life; this is the fine print of the etheric contract.
That's why the system puts so much effort into religion to perpetuate this witchcraft, to very low and dense energies from beings that live outside of you. They are controlling our minds and energies…
Social engineering or social programming.
That surrender, that lack, that request is what generates the contract.
Eduardo Coletto usually calls it "praying to Saint Pirulo", hahaha, I love it.
This contract is the permission that you grant to be parasitized from other planes and to create etheric cords and etheric implants.

Since you now know all this, your life could get crazier, because they are nervous about you ceasing to feed them, so they start to push you around in your real life. This has a double edge; it is a fight, **a war is being waged in the astral plane that we are not seeing it,** but, let's start fighting against all these traps that do not allow us live.

You have to feel empowered, a being of light, a powerful being, without 'lacking' where what counts most is your will. Start taking charge of your life. The light being, the god, the angel, call it as you want, but in the end, the power is you, only if you value yourself.

I have a physical body, an etheric body, and a light body, all three-in-one inside me, and I feel whole here and now. You have to be like me, to cut off those etheric contracts and etheric cords. If you feel powerful you will burn them down, but you have to really believe it, you must have a lot of willpower. You have to become empowered, take charge and be responsible for your life in all of your bodies, be responsible for your thoughts and your emotions. Get rid of that lack, of that needy human being, asking and requesting those things or external beings to fix his life...
(How very sad, such little responsibility, such little worth, such little power; how they program us like this...)
I ACCEPT MYSELF, I LOVE MYSELF, I'M GOING TO DO WHAT'S IN MY HAND, BUT <u>I WON'T PRAY TO "*SAINT PIRULO*" ANYMORE</u>.

The etheric contract is easy to make, it is simply requested from the 'lack' in your mind. Watch out for your intrusive thoughts; we have to start cutting them off and rejecting them with force. I DO NOT CONSENT.

3 THE INTRUSIONS

The intrusions, or interferences, actually they are a form of abuse, it depends on how you see it...
We have already seen the five bodies of the human being, and we must be very clear about this and be conscious at all times about their existence. So let's analyze the intrusions regarding to the human being's bodies.

Physical body:
Let´s think about when someone flicks you, or gives you a minor touch when talking to you. I don't really like those certain pokes from people talking to me. For example, when someone gets way too close while talking to you, so close that you can even smell their breath. We have a certain distance called a personal space bubble that we should always respect.

We must have a particular temper to not get affected by these situations, but it comes in handy if you can spot physical intrusions.

Mental body:
INSTRUSIVE THOUGHTS, interferences in our present, like when you are making mayonnaise and your mind suddenly starts thinking -without your consent- that you will cut your finger with the blender, that you will lose a finger. (Not to mention those radiation patents that we know about.)

They can also manifest in the form of paranoia. For example, you and your girlfriend are hanging out with another guy and you can see they get along great, so your jealousy gets activated. If you do listen to your mind, and if you do believe what it is thinking... this could start a fight due to those intrusive thoughts which could lead to problems with both of them, your girlfriend and the guy. It is crucial to spot this, because we were in moments of lucidity, living in our present, and suddenly our mind started thinking, producing intrusive thoughts and we abandoned our present.
Another good example is while on your phone, you don't see the profile picture of someone you really like anymore. The first intrusive thought is that he or she blocked you and deleted your contact. This happened to me, but it was because my friend got her phone robbed and lost all of her contacts.

Emotional body:
INTRUSIVE FEELINGS
For example, you are with your girlfriend and she says that you will both have dinner with her girlfriends. One of them is really pretty. We sit at the table, and some desires become activated in yourself...we have to be able to spot these intrusive feelings. The physical body, through the eyes, has triggered the emotional body, which has activated the desire. All of this comes from the outside, an external force. We must be conscious of this and be a true magician, a true magician in our inner self.

Here we can have two results: one, that you detect the desire, and calm yourself; or, you might not be conscious about these intrusions and finally you end up having a conflict with your girlfriend or her friend.

Energetic body:
INTRUSIVE ENERGIES
This has a lot to do with the energetic drainages. I remember, a long time ago, I had had a perfect day: I had a girlfriend, a job, nothing was lacking in my life. I was at home, and I felt a strange atmosphere, like my frequencies getting low with a very dense ambiance. I started feeling ill without any physical reason, without any mental reason, and without any emotional reason. It was due to the energetic plane, and I noticed what was really happening. We need to know how to spot this. We have already seen a brief explanation of what directed energy attacks are, or all of the radiation that is present in the environment, or other beings…

Another example of energetic intrusions are ENERGETIC PUNCHES (like psychic attacks). For example, when we are arguing with our partner, quite often things are not said in a respectful manner, and if we are hypersensitive, this will affect us considerably. This pain is an energetic pain, where the energetic drainages are produced. Further on, there is a whole chapter about these drainages.

Spiritual body or light body:
THE SPIRIT CAN NEVER BE INTERFERED
The spirit has everything, it can't be interfered.
It does not need anything or anyone. That outburst that we have, that inner force, it has everything, it is eternal and that's why it is not changing, that's why it never perishes.

From now on, the responsibility of spotting these intrusions in all of your bodies is on you. Always keep in mind the physical body, the mental body, the emotional body, the energetic body and the spiritual body. It's time for you to start feeling yourself and to start recognizing yourself. Mainly it's time for you to take the reins of your life in a conscious manner. It's time to leave the subconscious world in which we have been caged all our life.

By the way, there are also healthy intrusions, not everything is bad:

Physical body:
For example, when someone tickles you, or gives you a massage, etc.

Mental body:
For example, your brain appreciating what is being taught to you.

Emotional body:
For example, realizing how healthy and honorable your heart is feeling, without perversion.

Energetic body:
For example, feeling pure and pleasant energies for yourself, not those energetic punches mentioned before.

Spiritual body or light body:
It is always enlightened and giving light; another thing is that you may ignore it.

We all enjoy pleasantries and kindness, I believe.

I am going to tell you that all extremes are wrong - if you have very toxic intrusions or very negative ones, they are draining you. Likewise, if you have euphoric intrusions, you are being drained there as well. That's why the football fields are just like real energy batteries. You have half of it euphoric when their team scores a goal, and the other half, heart-broken and devasted when their team couldn´t save the goal. People are unaware of this, but in the astral plane, there are beings feasting on this. **When you see everybody doing something, ask yourself which trap lays behind, one that you don't see.** The fact that everybody drinks coffee falls under the same idea - ask yourself the reason why; or why does everybody drink certain drink? These are all physical deceits and hoaxes of the Matrix, which has an energetic background that we don't see.

I will leave you a blank page if you want to write any insights, learnings or anything else that caught your attention:

5 THE ARCHONS

First of all, I would like you to search for THE RADIOELECTRIC SPECTRUM; yes, there's a reason why it's called a spectrum. In it, you will observe that the frequencies visible to a human being are around 10^{15}. In other words, the segment between infrared rays and ultraviolet rays. We don't see wifi waves or any other type of electromagnetic radiation. Actually, a human being is relatively poor with his eyes so he can't see anything. That's why I'm telling you that there are so many things that we don't see - that surpass our reach, but here I am to uncover those beings that control us through the receptive pineal gland.

Have you ever felt, whilst in your house cleaning, or just being calm, as if someone was watching you and consequently you turned around? I'm sure that you have felt some sort of presence like this, like if you were accompanied while alone. It is them, these beings are there but our poor eyes can't see anything. If it happens to you again, it would be good that you pay attention to your energetic body and don't let your frequencies go down to inadequate densities because they will drain you.

For those who practice astral travels, you have undoubtedly seen them; they are like shadows, like Nazguls from The Lord of the Rings, or like Gollum in the dark. They feed on all evil and suffering.

I'm sure that also on some occasions, you have seen a shadow through the corner of your eye, like someone passing by; then you looked and there was nobody. You can see more frequencies with the corner of your eye, as Tesla has already taught us.

Only by mentioning the word *archons*, I have goosebumps, in a bad way, a bad feeling. The less we say that word, the better. Sometimes they are seen in this physical plane, especially around some mountains or hills; in the dark and with full moon, they allow themselves to be seen more. In the astral plane they have the habit of eating in energetic wells, which are generated through wars and deaths. That's the reason why there are so many wars in the world. If you have studied the XIX century wars you will know that none of those wars made sense. There was one after another and it was blatantly evident.

To detect archons parasitism is easy. When they parasitize, it results in people being wearisome, annoying, and insistent. You can also spot archons parasitism in human beings if the person is complaining all day. The archons parasitism is based on crying and sorrow. People become fragile human beings. For example, they also wish for others' failure, in other words, they are not happy for other people's success. People that do not contribute, that do not nourish others, people that criticize, and on top of that, they talk without setting an example... that is parasitism by archons.
There is always a way to say things in a good manner...
They usually don't have goals, they are afraid of change, they have fears. When someone is afraid of

something, serious or derisory, in that very moment of fear, they have one or various archons behind them, at their back, draining their energetic body, followed by goosebumps.

They tend to be eager to victimize themselves at high levels; they have serious ego problems; I can't understand why they don't know how to practice detachment.

That's why the world is how it is now, people all day long working, stressed, working too hard, and for what? Fifty years later, and you are still in debt. You grieve, and it has been fifty years feeding all of these beings. That's the reason why the world has been made like this; there is another dimension that we don't see.

You know it perfectly, you arrive home and you feel off, like something is missing, IT IS BECAUSE WE STOPPED BEING NATURAL. And the worst part is that these beings feed on us from other planes, our energetic body gets drained, and therefore we age faster.

Which side are you on?
Are you on the darkness' side or are you on the light's side?
Are you a cancer cell or an immunological cell?
Do you spend the day crying or do you spend it strongly facing your life with confidence?
Do you spend the day with fears and distrust?

Maite, my mother, has always told to me:

DARKNESS CAN ONLY BE DEFEATED IN ONE WAY, WITH MORE LIGHT

For us, light is information. For instance, if you are in a dark room, you will have certain fears like bumping into something, like your bed or the table, etc. Therefore, the metaphor of darkness is actually the lack of information. However, with this book you will have a lot of information or light.

The parasitism by archons, especially occurs in people who vibrate into the past, and we already said that the past is sadness and melancholy. Some of the arguments I had in my past relationships were due to my girlfriends vibrating in the past, they lowered their frequencies until the frequencies became dense. The archon can do whatever he wants with the human being, especially if the human is not conscious about his or her intrusive thoughts.

We must see the archon as the puppeteer, and see the human being, as the puppet.
Sometimes the parasitism is so complete, so profound, that the puppeteer becomes the puppet, the archon becomes the human being, and parasitism has won completely. An example of this complete parasitism is when the human being yells, gets enraged causing a sub-realist (surrealist) scene of being totally out of control.

¿Do you really think that your spirit is like this or would do something like this?

YOU ARE HARMING YOUR SPIRIT WHEN YOU ARE AFRAID, WHEN YOU ARE CRYING, WHEN YOU ARE FULL OF SORROW, AND ON TOP OF THAT, ALL OF THIS IS MAKING YOU AGE FASTER. YOUR SPIRIT IS THE OPPOSITE OF THIS, IT IS INFINITE, GRANDIOSE, WITH CHARACTER AND BURST.

There are different archons: small ones, medium ones and sergeant ones. Depending on their size, the parasitism is rougher.

WRATH
FEAR
TERROR
DOUBTS
DISTRUST
VIOLENCE – TO HURT
SHOUTING

They are really good at creating doubts in the human being's mind; beware that it is them doing so, especially if they are unhealthy doubts or negative doubts. This is produced through the pineal gland from other planes.

I will explain some cases where I suffered from archons parasitism. I should specify that it was not me being parasitized, but other humans I was close with who were parasitized.

I was in one of the best ecovillages of Alicante: Masambala. We spent some good days there, but one day, I was goofing around having fun with a water bottle. Alicante in the summer can reach temperatures of around 40-45ºC; so to be honest, if someone splashed me with cold water in such hot weather, I would appreciate that. The thing is, I was splashing some freshness (cold water) to other people, until I splashed the wrong person. That girl looked as if butter wouldn't melt in her mouth, like a harmless dreamy girl. (Turns out that, after joinging the ecovillage with her boyfriend, she had hooked up with some guys in just a few weeks; so be careful with two-faced people because they are the worst.) So, I lifted the bottle over her and I remember two drops of water falling on her, one on her forehead and the other one on her neck. Her face suddenly turned serious, staring at me. She was giving me a dirty look, she looked like she could kill me. I told her: ´Do you realize you are being parasitized, right?´

It didn´t change anything. She acted like an angry 3-year-old girl. I practice a lot of martial arts, so I just stayed there checking where was she going and what was she going to do. She stood next to me, on my right side, and in one second, she raised her arm and powerfully slapped my right arm with all of her power. Seriously, she hit me with all of her force; I knew she hurt her hand due to the roughness with which she slapped me. I was pretty amazed, thinking that this reaction couldn't be proportioned to the two drops of water (especially in a temperature of 45ºC), it was surreal. I put the cap back on the bottle, left it on the table, and told everyone: 'Hey, I'm going somewhere else because you don´t have a very peaceful energy here.´

Through the subconscious, archons take the totality of your body as you just have seen. Even the physical body as she came and slapped me.

Let's continue with another case: still in Masambala, that super fantastic ecovillage. It was still 45ºC heat, I got a nice tan, but I also got sunburnt, badly, with blisters. Let me paint a picture for you, my back was completely red; you could see it a mile off that I had been badly sunburned, and as you got closer, you could see those white blisters on my trapezius. I knew this, because people told me they could see it.
I like to help, so I was doing the dishes; and suddenly, out of the blue, without asking for it, I felt in my back a brutal relentless clapping on my blisters in one of my trapezius, very fast, more or less at a 400 km/h speed. I turn around, and I see a petite Argentinean girl, who has a kid (she's a mother), with a wooden spoon in her hand.
Honestly, I wanted to slap her so bad, but I don't hit women. So I took a deep breath, because she had clearly hurt me so badly physically (physical intrusion). I asked her why she had done that, if she could see a mile off that I had sunburn with blisters. She just smiled at me... I got closer, intimidating her a little bit, and told her not to do it again or else we would have a problem, to not touch me even with a stick, and I went back to do the dishes.

At this point, I want you to try stepping into my shoes, because at this moment of my life I can see people being puppets of these entities. The more empowered you get, the better you live your everyday life, as I do, VIBRATING INSIDE OF ME IN STATES OF LUCIDITY AND VIBRATING IN THE PRESENT. They need to use weak people from the outside to hurt me because internally, that pain that I was subconsciously doing to myself does not occur anymore.

Do you think your spirit would become empowered if you hit a human being 400 times in his sunburnt back and hurt him? Do you really believe that your spirit, which is the brightest part of you, will become empowered and tell you "Hey, you see that guy with the burnt back? Go slap him and break him!", like this, out of the blue, without that guy doing anything at all to you?
That's clearly a subconscious behavior, it would never cross my mind to do that, even less so if the guy hadn´t done anything to me. At this point it is more than clear that we are facing a clone, lacking of spirit and soul, just empty containers...

HOW TO AVOID ARCHONS PARASITISM?

First of all, you have to be a master of the mental body. Spend enough time in deprogramming and reprogramming yourself, or in other words, be at the point where you have deactivated certain

neuronal circuits and activated others to the point where you are a completely improved being. The point where you are someone very different to the one you were years before, and where you already have a good level of knowledge in neuroscience and epigenetics.
You need to log many flight hours, detecting the subconscious and detecting all of these mechanisms that occur in our interior.

Our biggest challenge is **shouting**. Search for something in your life that makes you want to shout and face the circumstances with an activated consciousness, knowing that it will want to make you burst out in anger. In my case, it happened many times with my father; I always talked to him about certain conspiracy theories and he reacted like a good ´sheeple´, a fact that I will never understand. Things always turned out badly for us and we always ended up shouting at each other. So one day I approached him, knowing that our energies would get turbid because he is weak and does not have the knowledge. He gets parasitized very quickly... we would end up arguing. Only this time, I had an understanding of this and I was going to practice it with an activated consciousness.
Sometimes, I would talk with my father about various topics, and we wouldn´t shout at each other at all, not once. However, other times, I saw that he said or did something to hurt me, but this time my mental subconscious and emotional impulse were controlled by my consciousness and spirit. I always had a paternal absence, also known as lacking a father figure. He always said that I was the worst and he never supported me, etc but it was with him who I practiced the consciousness the most, and I did a lot of inner work. Currently, we are not on such bad terms and that's an accomplishment. Every cloud has a silver lining.
The worst part of the human being is that it is a creature of habit. If you get used to shouting at your partner four times a week, you can both become masters in arguing four times a week. The week where you don't argue, you will end up seriously missing having arguments, even if after having the argument you both feel bad and you didn't mean to have it. That's why we need to be masters of our present, and be conscious. The Matrix program of the habit is quite dangerous, especially if it is about arguments that wear you down and drain you. We become true masters of what we do, so we need to acquire more responsibility for everything. I feel so ashamed when I see people my age behaving like brats. Social programming has activated the infantilization of the population in a terrible manner.
The power of getting used to bad things, OUT OF HABIT, is a very archon thing, that's why we have *Stockholm syndrome* - where the victim falls in love with their jailer or abuser. The worst part, is that there are people that can become **real masters** of vibrating in very low frequencies, like the frequency of slavery. And even worse, if they spend enough time there, when they finally get out of that situation, then they will miss those negative feelings, simply out of habit...

6 LOS LYONELS

I'm telling you once again, go to Google Images and search the electromagnetic spectrum and you will see that indeed the human being can only see a very reduced range of all of the frequencies that exist in 10^{15}, so we are genuinely blind. There are also Extremely Low Frequencies (ELF) waves ranging from 1Hz to 1KHz. If you research this, you will find that the human brain can be sabotaged and that brain waves work between 1Hz and 20Hz. For example, if they do radiate the following frequencies to us, they will produce:

6,6Hz – Depression
7,83Hz – Wellness
10,80Hz – Aggressiveness

These frequencies can be perfectly emitted either by beings from other planes or by certain atmospheric radiation and certain antennas. Now maybe you will understand why everybody is so furious or aggressive. As if they could choose, consciously... To wake up humanity, we must know all of the frequency attacks that we can suffer, and realize that we can have intrusions. The key is to work our subconsciousness and our consciousness.

Without further ado, let's see the "lyonel" kind. They look like the archons on the astral plane, but with some hound appearance, like ghost dogs, they walk on all fours. There are not many of them so they are difficult to see.

I would like to analyze the social programming that we have suffered since we were kids. For example, in The Lion King movie, the king of the jungle is the strongest one and he lives on that rock above the rest. That programming is very dangerous; putting ourselves above others. On top of that, they bomb us with that programming when we are just kids, when we are like sponges absorbing knowledge. The same example goes with John Rambo or Terminator, who make us feel as if we could end everybody by ourselves. And to have police that abuse the people, we have RoboCOP... We must break free from this installed programming, deprogram it. Delete old neuronal circuits and install some "more peaceful" ones.

Many girls and women get parasitized with the strong desire to control everything. I even heard, from a friend's girlfriend: 'Who is wearing the trousers in this relationship? Huh? I do!'

This is a clear example of parasitism by a lyonel. I have a female friend, who invited another female friend to live with her during the lockdown. In general, if you do this, you cannot reproach her for anything, because it was you that opened the doors of your home to her, and you invited her. Well, I ended up seeing this friend telling her "guest": 'It's me who brings in the money and everything else, you are living thanks to me!´

This is not logical, to invite your friend to stay with you, and then tell her that! It would have been better not to have invited her in the first place. That confrontational sentence revealing an "I am better than you" attitude, or "you are insignificant, you don't do anything, I do everything", is parasitism by a lyonel. In the moment where we launch an energetic punch, stepping on our friend, a lyonel or a ghost dog is behind us feeding on our energetic body. On top of that, the other party (our friend) will feel bad as well, and this can activate the parasitism by archons since there is guilt and a wound present in the situation. A lyonel can call and bring on more archons.

If these friends keep arguing unconsciously, we have quite a serious feast for beings in other planes. The worst part is, if we have constant daily arguments in the same places because the energy of that place gets corrupted, then negative astral portals can be created and used by those beings. These are created by having arguments many times in the same place, every day, during months or years. All of those arguments are unconscious, this being due to the lack of knowledge in psychology, neuroscience and epigenetics of the people having the argument; or, due to pure ignorance about life. I insist, we must watch out and be more attentive and aware of our energetic bodies.

If during a strong argument, you already have read this book and know all this, you are remembering about all of these parasitisms and that we all have an energetic body, which is the almost daily food for those beings. Therefore, you back off during the argument... that will be the first time that you eliminate a lyonel from the astral plane with the light of your spirit, activating the consciousness or your light body in that precise moment. Yes, you heard correctly, this is a way to eliminate them, with your consciousness, with your spirit, with an activated light body.

When you want to clear things up, it is difficult to back off in a tranquil and conscious manner but this is one of the secrets of the **magician** we have inside us.

If we are all captains of the same boat, there won't be parasitism by lyonels; in other words, if in a relationship, one ceases to be captain and becomes a marshal, in that case, there would be parasitism by lyonel due to that "*I command and you obey*" attitude.

If someone is so eager to talk the whole time, like a parrot, that is pure desire of playing the leading role, the need of standing out, ´**here I am´ is parasitism by lyonels**, it is anxiety. Sometimes it is good to shut these people up, but with consciousness, not just shouting ´Shut up! Shut up!´ - to them; it shouldn´t be like this.

The parasitism by lyonels can also be detected with guilt: "it was you, you, no one else..." If that person (is always accusing and blaming others) were conscious, we would sit down, and we would talk about the problem as adults - grown ups with some logged flight hours and kilometers on the road. There is too much childishness and immaturity in this society.

The interesting part about lyonels, is that you almost can´t see them, they access your pineal gland, like the others, that's why these are parasitisms. When they access, they activate your ego. The ego is placed in the emotional body, so be careful of that! If you offend me, you will die... So that is the problem, that they activate the ego, we listen to it, and we even believe it is us who thinks that way. No. People who feel above the rest, who never back off, surely have one or even three lyonels, meaning that they will have a severe problem with their energetic body. They are also not good at practicing humility.

All of our inner problems always occur for the same reasons:
1) There is an inner activation or an inner impulse
2) There is an inner listening
3) There is faith that what we are hearing is the supreme truth
I don't care if it is the physical, mental, emotional, energetic body... it is always like this. This programming, this 1,2,3 pattern. I hope you realise that this is total subconsciousness, bish, bash, bosh. There is no processing or even meditation, just impulses.

The attacks by lyonels are quite harmful to their victims in their energetic body...it is like a lion bite temporarily rupturing and bursting our energetic body.

Usually, people with feelings of inferiority need to step on the other people to feel above the rest. I sincerely do not understand this feeling of inferiority, it is just not me...not feeling superior, or above the rest...
They could be suffering from past traumas, like a family separation...
The more difficult a consciousness test is, the bigger the results you will have.
I want to cheer you up if you have had a lot of shocks in your life, because this means you had a more difficult test, and due to the inner wounds that you have, your subconscious will become triggered. Imagine if those beings are feeding on you or not. Now the responsibility is more considerable. This is a big topic, I know.

It is called parasitism by lyonels because you end up in the lion's claws... a lyonel is highly related with the ego and the emotional impulse from your heart...and it has a very strong activation.
Also, all of this gets multiplied thanks to his friends the archons.

There are many people that have detached themselves from their ego, so many beings have stopped feeding on them. For this reason, you don't see many of them in the astral plane, the ego has decreased. Watch out for tiresome people and people who blab, be careful.
This can be cured with humility, respecting others´ turns to speak, respecting others´ lives.

The hardest thing is the energetic body, and it is the ultimate aim for a lyonel, you will see. If you go to sleep with a damaged, energetic body, they feed on you while you are sleeping. You won't understand the physical attacks of lyonels, neither will you understand the mental or the emotional ones. But something you will understand to be an attack by lyonels, is that it is quite strong and quite hard, the pain will persist through the days or weeks, but this differs depending on the individual.

It is important to be cautious about these superiorities that can stalk any one of us, and to remember to push the "back off" button.

When you confront somebody parasitized by lyonels with their problems, most of them don't want to admit it. They escape the confrontation with their own problems, they shut down any dialogue. I remember that blonde girl, she was pretty parasitized by lyonels, she was always the one calling the shots, the one making the decisions, like she was the boss. When you are a victim of people like that, you end up feeling like you don't mean anything or you have nothing to do with her world or even with your own world. I remember telling her – I am not your fucking poodle lap dog please, you don't see *me*, you take me for granted…

Something just came to my mind: I remember that time when she was recklessly driving her car, wanting to inject me with fear, or to make a point that I was nobody and she was the boss.

Other times, for example, she wouldn't let me out of her house when I really wanted to leave. She had an eagerness to command and an attitude to put me in the position of a slave, not free, that is parasitism by lyonels.

If there is a suicide attempt, like the one she made me go through - hanging herself with the shower cord, emotionally and mentally blackmailing me so I would obey as a good slave - that is parasitism by lyonels, reptiles and archons.

I remember, in the summertime, she was asking me to go to sleep early every night because she had to work the next day; but when her male friend from Portugal came to visit one Thursday, she had bought a bottle of rum and orange juice. They were hanging out in the kitchen until 5 am. That subjugation that she had inflicted in me, forcing me to go to sleep early, ordering me with a baton. But then there was liberation…according to her command that Thursday, even though she had to work the next day, is parasitism by lyonels.

People parasitized by lyonels usually don't see their own mistakes, **there is no way they will do that!**
They are the king of the jungle, they do not pass through that process at all, they are superior.
When they force you to feel inferior, or when they humiliate you, be careful, it's them.

7 THE GRAYS

Search again on Google an image of the electromagnetic spectrum or the radioelectric spectrum - so we have this very clear, a human being can see frequencies of 10^{15} and can't see any further from that. This is the range between infrared rays and ultraviolet rays. The human brain works in ELF, Extremely Low Frequencies; specifically, from 1Hrz to 20Hrz.

The grays are like a typical alien, big heads, big eyes, with no mouth (as they don't need it) and they communicate telepathically. We have the grays and the tall grays. It is said that they are **clones** of reptiles. The grays do not feel or suffer, they are the most inert of all, they are **really empty beings.** The archons are the most 'animalistic' ones … (or wild), like the lyonels. But the grays are not so animal-like, not so wild; even though they are so empty because they lack an emotional body. They have no scruples, are very intelligent and energetically strong.
I didn't see them in the astral, but where I did see them was in dreams…where abductions take place and implants placed in you while you are resting…

How can I spot them? You must be asking. Well, they are expert energetic masters, they can move energies to perfection. Without moving a finger, they can cause you a big energetic problem. I am going to show you some examples so you understand what I mean.

I remember, one late afternoon I was sitting at my desk, in front of my computer… I didn't have any reason to feel bad - I was doing well with my girlfriend, with my job and with my family etc. Well, I started feeling so weird, like the ambiance was turning on an energetic level. As each minute went by, everything was feeling more and more dense, like that feeling of being underwater. I started feeling bad without any reason, and I noticed something… shoot, what is happening to me? I was wondering for ages until I realized… I realized it was 'them', trying to sabotage me from other planes, to feed themselves on my energetic body. If you do not know this, you start to feel not so good because you are in the frequencies of sorrows and evil, and archons are eating you from other planes. However, I stopped it, because I am conscious of all of these types of evil intrusions that we can suffer, that **drag us out of our valuable present time.**
The problem, besides feeling those energies from those very strong grays, is if you listen to them and believe them to be true. You fall into their game, their trap and you start to feel negatively without knowing why…

I caught them because, physically, I was feeling good, at my best, due to the training. Mentally and emotionally, I was good too, I had no problems. The spirit is always good, but the attack of the grays is produced in the energetic body so be careful. It is not pineal like in the other examples before that were based on archon´s evil madness or the lyonel´s ego.

Another hard example of a gray´s or tall gray´s attack is sleep paralysis. If you have suffered from sleep paralysis or still suffer from it, you should know it´s them. They make you feel bad, and in the astral plane, archons and other beings will be able to see this, so they will come to feed on your energetic body. The sooner you can see this, the sooner you will wake up like Neo did in the Matrix when he comes out of the red capsule and sees the energetic world that he was not able to see before, but that he was able to perceive and feel.

The last time that I suffered from sleep paralysis was at the end of summer 2020, just days after the parasitism by lyonels was passed from the blonde girl to me...the girl who took me for granted, who didn't value me? Could these have been related...?

I remember being in bed, and felt like a hand was grabbing my ankle, squeezing it, and pulling it down abruptly, waking me up, AHHH! Within that second, I knew it was them, because I couldn't move in my bed but I was awake. I usually exercise a lot with kyokushinkai, taekwondo, chin-ups etc - they really helped me that night. I was hugging the sheets with the idea of feeling very comfortable already in my mind so I could sleep pleasantly. So, I said to myself, ´I´m going to sleep so well!´. By not giving them attention, and not being a victim of fear, they got angry. They moved me from my left shoulder to right foot, quite a pirouette. I acted like nothing happened and kept with my idea of being comfortable and in control. So, they moved me again and left me as I was before in my initial position. Now it was time to make me do the same pirouette, but in reverse: from my right shoulder to left foot. However, I kept doing my thing, with the determination to sleep. Then they left me alone. I couldn't move, like I was under a spell. If you try to move your physical body, you will get scared because you can't, so it is better to ignore the physical body. If we can control our mind, that's better, as I did. Emotionally speaking I gave a hard pass on everything because I wanted to sleep after my workout. At an energetic level, I was calm, vibrating in comfort and wanting to sleep.

They were attacking me for a little while more and finally they declared me invalid. **They had spent too much energy on me.**

This trick is what really makes them leave you alone for a while. If you fall prey to their claws, if you fall under their spell, most surely they will come back wanting to feed themselves because they know it worked last time.

If they do this to a person that does not know anything about them, and who falls into the trap of fear and terror, which is the ultimate goal for them, it is there where they can see your rotten energetic in the astral plane. Moreover, archons and other beings that we can't see jump out to feed themselves. On you. That's why I'm telling you, that the more you know, the lighter you are. Information is light, and it is created when one is wise and practices what he has learned.

Mainly, the grays attack during REM sleep. They generate nightmares of terror and fear, or they make sure that we suffer from feeling scared. They are experts in frequencies, especially in our brain's frequencies in order to manipulate us:

0,5Hz – 4Hz DELTA activity:
We enter the DELTA state when we are asleep or unconscious.
Children from 1 to 2 years old when awake are in DELTA state.

4Hz – 8Hz THETA activity:
We enter the THETA state when we create or invent something.
Children from 2 to 6 years old are in DELTA and THETA states.
(Hypnosis is produced in DELTA and THETA). The subconscious, children from 2 to 6 years old, exactly when we are more indoctrinated or taught...that is not an education. The brain in DELTA and THETA states, besides being a creator, is really able to assimilate a lot of complex information.

8Hz – 12Hz ALFA activity:
We enter the ALFA state when for example we are in a stressful situation, we stop and WE TAKE A BREATH: AAAAAAaaaaaahhhh. That breath, that pause, is the most important thing to detect intrusive thoughts and to detect the entire subconscious. It is what breaks the pattern of impulses, one after another, it is what breaks these programmed automatisms. ALFA is the maximum level of reception.

12Hz – 35Hz BETA activity:
We enter the BETA state when we pay conscious attention.

+35Hz GAMMA activity (the seventh sense)
We enter the GAMMA state when we reach the state of experimenting an absolute consciousness in all of its senses. When we verge on the divine limit and we really are supranatural.

If you feel great for several days, in the astral plane, it is like a big lantern getting bigger and bigger. However, you are good until they come and prepare something to extinguish that flame. They can't allow us to shine for a long period of time, we are their nourishment. When you know about this, they can't sabotage you via your subconsciousness because you control the mental subconscious, the emotional impulse, the energetic subconscious, etc. and they can't sabotage you from your interior. Most likely, they will use people close to you (friends and family...), parasitize them, transform them into their puppets and make them attack you. You will realize a lot of these kinds of things, or you are starting to realize already. They will use weak people around you, subconscious people, ignorant people, experts and masters in making subconscious actions or living their lives in a subconscious way. If they parasitize them with archons, action such as shouting will happen. If they parasitize them with lyonels, they will try to make you feel insignificant or they will humiliate you.

The grays are experts in inducing you all kind of energetic frequencies such as making you feel guilty. If you feel that energy of guilt, listen to it and believe it, most surely some memories on a mental and emotional level will become activated. In that situation, we would have the same situation of the subconsciousness working and actions taking place without our consent, one after another. A complete menu of intrusions, starting with intrusive energies, followed by intrusive feelings and after that, intrusive thoughts. I insist, that if we listen to all of that, we give power to it, and we believe it; the action following all of those automatisms will be a total subconscious action.

The problem we have here is that we are used to living our lives in a rush. We live a fast life, so we will act like this out of habit, rapidly and rushed. By living our lives this way, we will fall prey to automatisms time and time again.

We have now looked at the physical intrusions, the mental ones, the emotional ones; but these last ones, the energetic intrusions, are the most difficult of them all. This is because a process of learning is required, a certain mastery. First of all, we need to be masters of our physical body, then of our mental body, after that, we need to be masters of our emotional body and finally, masters of our energetic body. If we do this properly, our spirit will start to become stripped naked little by little, coming out more and more. Right now, all of the mental and emotional garbage is covering it up, the scourge of the subconsciousness is covering it.

PHYSICAL – MENTAL – EMOTIONAL – ENERGETIC – SPIRITUAL

The more we train the ALFA state activity in ourselves, by training the conscious breathing, giving us a break when we have mental or emotional saturation, the better. If we are able to be masters in ALFA brain activity, we will be able to not fall in the trap of rushing or automatic impulses. We will be able to dodge them or more simply we won't action them.

> The grays mainly make you lower the frequency of your being. They are really good in lowering your energy and from that point, they activate the subconsciousness of the other bodies (although in sleep paralysis they directly cut your access to your own physical body).

8 THE REPTILES

I insist, go to Google Images and search for the electromagnetic spectrum. There is a reason why it is called spectrum... there are shadows that we can't see.

How to detect parasitism by reptiles?
When you want to detect parasitism, you are already in the middle of their trap and it is too late. They are the most intelligent ones and the strongest ones. I always say that if you conduct astral travels, the best thing to do is to pretend that you didn't see those beings. However, if they are reptiles, get away from them!

Beware that they are reptiles, like a chameleon. Imagine that you have a dead uncle, in the astral plane they can appear with the appearance of your uncle and they can fool you. They also do these kinds of things in dreams. They are masters of camouflage, always in disguise ngmeani you won't see them...

According to Eduardo Coletto, the people that believe fervently in Jesus or Allah or in any other god for that matter, when they die and experience ´judgement day´, they will meet their god, and they will do anything their god requests drooling over their idol... Sad but true, a good etheric trap. Honestly, both Eduardo Coletto and I don't care about the explicit names of these interdimensional beings, if they are archons, reptiles or whatever, we don't care. The thing is that they are there. Often we call them other names such as "guachos", lizards, San Pirulos etc...

If anybody is following Eduardo Coletto, they will know that it is always the same story. They have the etheric body attached to a crown, with chains, a throne, a scarf, a dress or something. All of those are etheric implants, and they have the etheric body locked under these circumstances. On top of that, they pose as "friendly figures", but actually they are reptiles in disguise.
Be careful with the etheric plane, a lot of "figures" can be a disguise.

Reptiles build complicated strategies, and you only realize it when it´s too late.
The pain that reptiles cause comes with poison, they poison you for a while after they strike Your mental, emotional and energetic bodies will keep hurting. The pain is able to reach your spirit. For example, they played a trick on me, exposing my picture through humiliating memes amongst other things such as stalking and just wreaking havoc on my life. The reptiles used a lot of weak people to attack me. I couldn´t sleep for five days, and I was feeling bad for 2 weeks. I can see a lot of puppet people, without power, but wishing for evil things to happen to others. If someone says A, all of them, like sheeple, will go to A. If someone else says B, all the sheeple will go to B.

This attack took place because I was exposing a lot of the topics that I am explaining today in this book online. Most likely, they will prepare some mega strategy against me for depicting everything I know about them in a paper book format and PDF in Spanish and English. **But I am not afraid. I think it is time**

to wake up, like Neo did in The Matrix, and start to see this energetic consumption that we suffer on a daily basis. I insist that this is the key to everything, being aware of our energetic body and realizing the drainages.

The most important thing is to PROCESS INFORMATION, to write it, study it, see it and put it into practice. We must be true masters at detecting intrusions.

MASTERS IN DETECTING INTRUSIONS:
If we are a white belt in detecting intrusions, and this is the first time that we have worked on this, it´s really quite late and we will have to seriously roll up our sleeves. This is because most surely, we will detect them as the days go by, meaning that we are late as they have already happened.
If we are a brown belt in detecting intrusions, we can sometimes catch them when they are happening - in that very instant, but at other times maybe we will miss them and instead, we will detect them after a few minutes or hours have passed. We must polish the technique and get better. What we are aiming for is to detect them ipso facto, at the very second that they appear.
After some years, you are more prepared, and you can spot them before they come; we are really aiming for that level of awareness – of being able to see them before they happen.

MASTERS IN ACTUATION, WHEN YOU CAN MAKE THE CLICK:
Once the intrusions are clear, then we have to activate our microcosm.

These switches will be on the **physical** plane, on the **mental** plane, on the **emotional** plane and/or on the **energetic** plane. I'm talking about operating in the **subconscious** in order to deactivate it and activate the consciousness. In other words, this would be deactivating old neuronal circuits in order to activate other new ones.

The reptiles can present themselves in the physical plane. Many people see figures or shapes at home, when they go to sleep, or when waking up. But they are always wearing a disguise, you will never see them in their original shape. They do this so there is never the same testimony about seeing a reptile. For example, my brother saw a fisherman, like the one in the movie *'I know what you did the last summer'*. He had a really bad time and was scared when it started appearing by his bed. He never did anything to my brother, and he was already a teenager when that happened to him.
It will always be a reptile in disguise, different figures every time.

When the time karmic judgement comes, we should tell them to wear no disguise, to take it off, and then we ignore them, because we don't want to establish a contract with anybody.

When people pray to an outside being, we are making an etheric contract with them. In the moment where we are vibrating outside ourselves, we can, in some way, be interfered by them. This is the most important thing in the world: to vibrate inside of ourselves and with states of lucidity. We shouldn´t vibrate in the past (as it causes melancholy and sadness) and not to vibrate in the future (as it causes anxiety).

The most dangerous thing is that, some people, for example, have a dead uncle, and they vibrate outside of themselves, very far away, so the interferences can occur easily in an etheric manner. Nobody -not even them- know where that dead uncle may be, the idea is very confusing, and they -the reptiles- take advantage of that from the astral plane or etheric plane. Also we should note that, they are also vibrating in the energy of death… Consequently we have unconscious human beings, vibrating outside of themselves and on top of that with the energy of death.
I think we can call this witchcraft… WE HAVE UNCONSCIOUS HUMAN BEINGS VIBRATING OUTSIDE OF THEMSELVES, AND WITH THE ENERGY OF DEATH…

Surely an etheric contract will be generated unconsciously. We already said that this contract will come with a surprise, with a fine print.
It is normal that strange things happen to people, or they are trapped in a loop, or wondering why such things happen to them, **or why everything happens the opposite way they want.** They are practising witchcraft daily or weekly, generating etheric contracts daily or weekly in a totally unconscious or subconscious manner. Those who do this every day have a big problem, (and people who do it every month as well); as they will have many surprises and surreal experiences…

I think that everything is becoming pretty clear that we should be vibrating inside of ourselves within a state of lucidity and vibrating in the present, not in the past or in the future.

WE MUST LET THE DEAD REST IN PEACE

Let go, practice detachment, be able to become detached in order to give…

A friend of mine, Ana, (a.k.a. Francia), is having a bad time and her three children have been taken away from her into foster care. Thanks to all of these teachings she now believes in herself, she is now empowered and she is stronger than ever. She feels very thankful. If someday you read this book, thank you Ana for listening to me and following my advice, now you are as free and as strong as I am.
She vibrated outside of herself many times, she vibrated in her children, and that's normal, but she has now corrected this. If someone does this, and on top of that, he or she vibrates in sorrow or any other negative energy, they are making etheric contracts for the poor children who know nothing about it. In other words, she was carrying out witchcraft on her children. (If only it was good energy…)

That's why there is so much social programming with religion. They will never tell believers to vibrate inside themselves in a state of lucidity, not in the past or in the future, and they won't tell them to believe in themselves, ever. **They will always point them towards the social programming of 'lacking**

something´ and asking superior beings to fix their life. We can't deny that from this point of view, the childishness and immaturity can't be more obvious.

None of them are able to take responsibility of their own life, they pass the responsibility onto those superior entities and we know how that turns out...

The arborescent thinking and the infinity of possibilities are important. The more information we have the less we will be fooled, like when the electric company scammers want to come inside our home....
We have to know how to NOT CONSENT.

The reptile parasitism increases the emotional charge considerably. They play the sorrow and the melancholy cards...and if it's related to dead people, their archon friends will probably come.
They can also manipulate you to make you do a bad action unconsciously, then they inject you with the feeling of guilt. If you do not control this, you will back feed on that and you will be trapped in a loop.
The etheric implants are placed by reptiles and grays. For example, if I have an etheric implant in my mouth, and you have an etheric implant in your ears, every time that you hear a word from me, the etheric implant will make you angry and most surely you will shout at me or attack me.
Every time that etheric contracts are generated, the reptiles have the right to be the surgeons of your body to inject you with these etheric implants. Sometimes you can feel when they are putting it in you, with a pain like a pin piercing deeply into your skin. However, sometimes you won't feel them so try to notice what I told you about the mouth-ears-anger effect. Detect your implants and the other people's implants.

We must stop making connections - don't connect yourself with the moon, or the sun, don't connect with anything, at least without knowing a single thing about your energetic body. Many people do these kinds of things out of ignorance.

Vibrating inside yourself, you must learn.

Be careful when you love (in Spanish "Amor", written backwards is "Roma") and... **All roads lead to Rome...**

Parasitism by a reptile can also be detected with lies, even small ones. In the very moment where the truth is changed even slightly, there is parasitism by a reptile. That's why it is said that there are people who are ´snakes´, liars. HALF-TRUTHS...
We can also detect parasitism by a reptile because there is normally an elaborate plan lingering in the background. For example, let´s think back to that blonde girl I spoke about before...one day we got angry with each other, then after that she was trying to seduce me for about three weeks. I finally went to see her... 500 Km away. What I didn't realise, is that I had fallen into her trap. Every night we had an argument, there was always some rivalry on her part. I couldn't understand why she seduced me for 21 days in a row, if then we had some conflict every day? I wouldn't do this to anyone, seducing someone

for 21 days, making them travel for 500 Km just to have an argument every night... I truly don't understand it. However, if we notice that there is a reptile behind this weak girl, we can understand it better...

Every night we had arguments (on her part), and afterwards she ended up telling me "come on, let's go to sleep", as if she were commanding it with a baton. (Parasitism by a lyonel as explained before.) On the third day, she was angry, telling me that she didn't trust me, that I was the worst, etc. That didn't add up, how can you seduce someone for three weeks to later on tell him these things? If you are able to see the reptile behind, orchestrating this elaborate plan, you will understand. **She was a simple puppet... like when agent Smith in the Matrix takes control of the lady in the red dress at the beginning of the movie**. I'm sure that his spirit, full of light, would never do something like that. A puppet person is not conscious about his or her high ego.

You can see puppet human beings, like when someone gets close with his or her abuser or jailer. This is Stockholm syndrome, and is why I can't talk anymore to that girl...

One more thing, archons carry the infinite negative energy, like wanting to kill, hurt, create violence, provoke suicide... they are masters in these energies. Reptiles consume the energy of the other extreme, the energy of the total euphoria. That's why there is a giant battery in the astral plane, in all the concerts or football stadiums. The potential difference that is generated in football fields when a team scores, half of the stadium feels so good and the other half feels so bad – this is the best built astral battery ever. Something really impressive, difficult to believe, but it makes sense when you start learning from Eduardo Coletto or Corrado Malanga.

The planet is under so much stress, so the archons can feed. Then these human beings get tired of feeling bad and need to loosen up, so they start drinking or taking drugs on the weekend. This plan deserves an applause; we are their food source, their animals, they can feed on us. Of course, let´s not forget about the energetic body and all of the drainages that we suffer.

Reptiles like to make you live and feel the infinity of the positive and the infinity of the negative. For example, when you meet somebody, a really special partner, and you live as if a dream had come true, floating, super high...get ready... you will also live some heavy and hard moments, surreal situations... both the extremes. If this happens with somebody, there are reptiles near, be aware to see how will they actuate and from where will they do it, so you can detect and actuate as well.

They also like to throw very clear mental flashes at you. They make you see nitid images taking you away from your present. They are very accurate, and powerful, it is them, the reptiles. (Take it as no laughing matter).

9 THE MANTIS

Let's begin as usual, considering the electromagnetic spectrum, where our eyes can't see a thing on the 10^{15} range and our brain works on the ELF frequencies range. This is from 1Hz to 20Hz approximately, even reaching more than 35Hz if we can achieve elevated states of consciousness.

On the astral plane, I haven't seen a mantis, but this can be due to their camouflage; notice how, on this physical plane, mantises can place themselves on a green leaf and we can't see them. Maybe they have some invisibility skills too.

Mantises can usually close your eyes, and kill your taste. Those human beings use an ideal moment of your life to get their hands on you. Their most notable feature is that they can induce you to have erotic dreams and even reach climax. As Eduardo Coletto has explained, this is done on the astral plane. It produces a bursting energy that beings of other planes can use for all kinds of investigations such as cloning on the ethereal plane. Mantises can activate your sexual desire to high levels. If this impulse reaches unhealthy levels, it's them manipulating you.

Did this happen to you? Having an orgasm while sleeping? This is textbook parasitism by mantises.
It is easy to detect parasitism by mantises in the physical plane. I'm sure that you may have a friend, male or female, that lives life as a slave in a sexual context. I mean, they can't be alone, they need to be with somebody. They don't value solitude, or silence, or peace. For example, I know a guy who people call "the womanizer"; and another female friend who is always horny. Mantises are also masters in parasitizing you with jealousy. Be careful, jealousy issues are managed by them!

Remember that any parasitism easily unbalances you and takes you out of your centre.

For example, it would also be a parasitism by mantises if there's something that makes you mentally **sick** on the physical plane. There are people who like to train and workout, and they become training **fanatics** until they become sickly obsessed. Anything that is an **insane addiction** is parasitism by mantises, especially addictions of a sexual nature. Other addictions such as smoking, drinking or drugs are also parasitism by mantises. What a coincidence that the system promotes tobacco and alcohol. During those lockdowns, tobacco shops were open, even though there was a pulmonary disease plaguing the world... There are people who prefer the after-sex cigarette more than actually having sex; these are the levels people can reach...
That's why food has so many additives, or can be addictive like chocolate or coffee. People have a serious disease when an addiction is produced in their unhealthy life. Furthermore, when your body tries to calm that addictive anxiety, it is then when the mantises on the energetic plane drain your energetic body. When you suffer the yearning of your addiction, you have some archons draining you, so it's a double attack. That's why I must stress that mantises kill you when you close your eyes in pleasure.
One of the biggest powers of mantises, is that they can steal almost all of your sacred energy. SEX in English stands for: **S**acred – **E**nergy – e**X**change
If you make love with someone who is heavily parasitized, you can fall into a big trap. I remember that I sometimes felt so empty, and it could take me half a year to recover that energy that I had lost or that someone had stolen from me.

10 THE LUX

In this trap we have all fallen, especially us people who are very good, kind and give so many opportunities to others, because they fool us or because we have some foolish hope. Many others have the social programming of *'new age do-goodism'*, like everything is good and fine, fantastic, total flower-power. I think you know what I'm talking about. On the astral plane those are light balls, be careful and don't be fooled.

People parasitized by lux deny their negative side, and we all have a negative side, all of us, and sometimes, when they push your buttons, we explode. If you are conscious of it, you explode in a way that doesn't harm that much, but if you do it in an unconscious way, you will explode in a manner where you can really harm others. Those people don't have the guts to talk about bad issues. They don't dare talk about their mistakes which is key in a relationship, In order to change and amend mistakes to improve, you must be able to see what´s wrong. It is okay to talk about what bothers you about your partner and vice versa. It is the first step to become supernatural, acceptance.

EVERYTHING THAT I KNOW ABOUT MY LIGHT MY DARKNESS TAUGHT ME
(In other words, in order to see the good, we must first see the evil)

Hegelian dialectic is a very important factor in social programming, based on only having two options, A and B. They limit and restrict us in all senses.

It is the antithesis and the thesis. For example, capitalism or communism; death or freedom. And the trap is set to have us in-between, like with political parties: republican or democrat, left-wing or right-wing. They limit our mind with A or B. Social engineering is pretty harsh. If for example they ask you right now, how would you improve a TV remote? Nothing would come to your mind, because social programming has activated your convergent hemisphere, so the divergent brain creativity has been cancelled. Ask that same question to a kid, and he will tell you a thousand ways to improve the TV remote. He will tell you A, B, C, D, … He won't stay just on A or B.
We also have to uninstall another program that we have in our minds, the one that wants us to save everyone else. This is a mistake, because we should first save ourselves from ourselves. If you have too much mental or emotional garbage, you won't save anybody; it will end up having the opposite effect: you will end up filling the people you want to help with your own garbage. So, in order to help others, at least first you can't have intrusive thoughts, intrusive emotions or intrusive energies. There are so many people around giving lessons when actually, they are not even comfortable with themselves when in solitude.

When you give a second chance to someone, even when you know that he or she doesn't deserve it: that is pure parasitism by lux. We can say that lux takes advantage of our kindness. Lux consumes and feeds on good energies. Parasitism by lux generates the beginning of the Stockholm syndrome. And after that, our other little friends that we now know will come to the feast, to eat you up when you realize that you shouldn't have given a second chance to that person. Lux makes us blind. It is pretty ridiculous and sad to see how they use our kindness while we fall intro the trap. **DO NOT CAST PEARLS BEFORE SWINE**. They don't deserve it, and we don't deserve it either.

11 THE CLONES AND THE SHEEPLE

I am sure that at least once in your life you have observed the particular actions of other people and it seemed like if they were empty inside, as if they don´t feel or suffer. I say this especially because nobody looks at the sky anymore; it's been so long since I saw a vivid blue sky, full of white, pompous 3D clouds, so spongy and fluffy that you feel like bouncing on the top of those clouds. I remember, when I was a kid, I could even see shapes and figures in those clouds and a vivid blue sky.

Clones, are not able to see the most obvious things that are happening right in front of them. You can even tell them a serious problem, such as a global one, and they will reply: "Yeah sure… but what can we do about it? What are you going to do? We can't do anything…¨

We can say, that they are the quitters, disinterested people that don't care about anything, and that nature related problems are not their problem. I warn you, that if someone doesn't care about nature, he won't care about you either; because the main form of empathy is empathy towards nature. If they don't care about this, they couldn't care less about your problems, so they won't have much empathy for anything that happens to you, they just mind their own business. Their business always comes first.

Dolly the sheep was cloned in 1996, on the 5th of July. If they publicly published this, it is because they had already been investigating this matter for several years, they had succeeded, and the sheep had lived for some years, she didn't die easily. This must have been the first investigation that succeed first time round. They said that this was in order to be able to feed the whole population; in fact, they already sell cloned meat and people have no idea about it. This goes for many tomatoes that I find in the supermarket, they all look the same and don't have any taste…like they have no essence at all.
By creating clones, they create beings without essence. They will have a physical body, yes, and you will see them, you will even be able to eat them. They will have a mental body and an emotional body too. But I highly doubt that they will have an energetic body and a spirit. In other words, I am sure that they don't have the essence of living beings. I disagree with eating meat or eating dead cells that experienced murder. However cloning goes one step further and completely breaks the spiritual and the energetic cycle. A clone didn´t come from a mother's womb, it doesn't have a family, and it doesn´t feel love from a father and a mother who gave it life… It is not produced in a natural way; it is not created with that natural explosive energy. And if it does not start in a natural way, then it starts in an unnatural way.
Do you now understand why people are always hungry? They are not feeding themselves in an energetic way. They do feed themselves physically, but not energetically.
I am sure that in 2020 you argued with people to the point that you even thought that you were not from the same species. Here's the answer; between clones and parasitized people, I believe that you now know more things about what happened to you and what will happen to you in life.

Nottingham University generated 4 Dolly clones in 2007. It is now 2021.
We have some very famous cases with humans:
Singer Avril Lavigne, rapper Eminem, our dear Paul Walker from "The Fast and the Furious" and even president Putin. If you search on Google Images the word "clone" followed by any of these mentioned names, you will quickly realize that what I'm saying is true.

There is a documentary about how they have injected clones into the population since 1939…

I will leave you a blank page if you want to write any insights, learnings or anything else that caught your attention:

12 ELIMINATE FEAR

I already said that in order to empower ourselves, the first thing is to follow the order of the five bodies:

PHYSICAL – MENTAL – EMOTIONAL – ENERGETIC – SPIRITUAL

Experts in martial arts like KYOKUSHINKAI and TAEKWONDO, won't have fear, because they will become real combat warriors.

Fear, is usually a very high state of consciousness, a very high state of reality. However, it becomes a serious problem when fed. For example, I think everybody has had fear, or the realist paranoia about someone breaking into your house. If these thoughts are daily, they are intrusive thoughts that take you away from the present and leave you with unhealthy energies.

I will explain my case to you; I saw the problem I had because almost every day I thought about it. So I took action. I wasn't like an ostrich who buries his head in the sand and can't see anything. I faced my problems and my fears. That's the first step, **to see it, accept it and face it.** I bought a baseball bat, which still lays on the left side of my night table. I remember that I was 18, and that summer, I signed up for KYOKUSHINKAI karate lessons and TAEKWONDO the following year. As the months and years passed by, I felt more powerful, stronger, faster and more flexible. This decreased the paranoia about people breaking into my house. Indeed, I don't like violence at all, and I had to make an effort to improve my martial arts. I remember my GOLDEN master told me to hit him harder, and I just couldn't do it...I couldn't think about doing that to my grandmaster. Then he said –"I'm your master! If you don't listen to me, that's an offense."

When I heard that, I hit him hard and I remember his face changed a little and he smiled at me... Since then, I started loosening up with everyone, and I understood that it was not violence. I realised that hitting hard was key for my partner to learn how to take hits. This is a psychosomatic effect that will pass from the physical body to the mental body and then to the emotional body. It took me four years to loosen up, and from there I started growing exponentially in my martial arts path. Even several masters told me to sign up to a national tournament, that I could win for sure.

After that, the virus of fear totally disappeared. I could go to the ATM and withdraw 300€ in notes without any fear because I knew at all times that if anything happened, the other one would be the one who got hurt...(the ones that would try to do wrong to me) and not me. I have lived with that feeling since then. I'm so dangerous in the physical plane that I really don't care about anything that could happen.

Occasionally, the intrusive thought about someone breaking into my house to steal appeared. So I decided to move to the 'next level'. I researched artisan *katanas* and bought one. I have it in front of my bed, on a stand, displayed, sharpened, polished, and I do the cleaning and oiling treatment every year.

However, that intrusive thought came back, stronger than before because I was worried that whoever broke into the house could carry a gun. So I wondered what I to get rid of this feeling. Since I am a "ninja", I searched for something silent. Therefore I got into bows, crossbows, and compound bows. I joined an archery range and liked it very much, so I bought myself a compound bow for about 600€. It also ´sleeps´ with me in my bedroom.

Nevertheless, despite this physical strengthening and house strengthening, the intrusive thought still came to my mind, and I was like... I have done everything I can. So I decided I wasn´t going to do anything else. I don't care; if it happens, it happens. I had reached a point where there were no excuses to be afraid.

SHEEP SPEND THEIR ENTIRE LIVES FEARING THE WOLF, BUT IT IS THE SHEPHERD WHO EATS THEM IN THE END

After all of that, up until now, I don't have that intrusive thought about a break-in anymore. Maybe someone, due to χ reason, needs more than me, or couldn't get what I have. So, the advice here is...take sufficient action depending on your circumstances. Get yourself a German shepherd for example, or get an alarm system installed with cameras and microphones, etc. However, you can't be spending everyday feeding archons!

Honestly, I didn't know that thinking someone could break into my house was an intrusive thought, but it is. Any thought that takes you away from your valuable present and intoxicates you is not healthy. It is an intrusive thought that doesn't belong to you. The ones that are not intrusive thoughts are the ones that calm you down. These thoughts encourage you to find solutions to calm your present and therefore promote healthier thoughts.

Another form into which fear manifests itself is from a lack of information or doubts. For example, when your girlfriend gets on really well with her male friend... When you were 15 this meant going crazy and having an argument. But now, at my age, when I feel jealous, I laugh about it because I know that it is these "guachos" as Eduardo Coletto calls them, (let's call them suckers). They are from other planes, trying (because they can't get away with it) to stop me from valuing my present. I have reached an evolutive moment where I accept everything that happens to me, and mainly I vibrate from within, in a lucid state, in the present, not the past or in the future. I will not vibrate in this jealous state... they can only wish. I have seen jealous people become very aggressive because they had those intrusive thoughts and THEY LISTENED TO THEM AND BELIEVED IT. This is where the energetic body gets activated and stops being human. They are puppets of all of those beings in other planes.
Another example is when someone is laughing at you, which also happened to me. I simply walked away, and that was it.
We came here to do this, to show you that you can be a magician inside of you, for you to understand that you can live in your present, in your life. By knowing that you can stop being a slave of all those traps, you can stop being a slave to unconscious life.

The biggest step for a human being is this one, **STOP BEING AFRAID, because it is this principle that is needed to evolve the energetic body.** A human being that is afraid, or having an argument, restarts his energetic body. Yes, you heard me correctly, when you are having an argument, or suffering any kind of fear or abuse, your energetic body decreases considerably. By decreasing, your aura also decreases, and consequently etheric implants from other planes can be installed. Beware that this is very serious matter.

The next step to not being afraid and feeling strong is food and nutrition. I see many 'carnivores' saying "you are what you eat, right". And I laugh... if you eat dead cells, blood, animals that have suffered in fear, murder and violence, this is the very same thing you have inside of you. Plus, at this point, we now know that some astral portals could be generated in our stomach meaning we could easily be parasitized.

What I just said is very logical. For example, if we prepare a freshly cut pineapple juice and drink it... a lot of chemical processes will be generated to digest that pineapple. Of course, pineapple is made up of living cells, and when you ingest living cells, you feel how your energetic body expands, and you feel more powerful. Fruit is really good. However, if you feed your stomach with blood, that is dead cells, cells that have lived through fear, terror and violence. It is clear that the final product won't be good if the raw material is death.

When I stopped eating meat, I stopped introducing blood, fear, terror, death and dead cells into my being. I felt noticeably different and had a fantastic change in all my senses. I have a very strict living cells diet 30 days a month, I mean, if I have to cheat one day on this diet it is okay since I know that I follow a good diet the rest of the year. It is good not to become obsessive or fanatic about things. For example, if there is a Christmas dinner with my company, I won't say anything and will in fact jump through hoops, especially if I was just hired recently. It is not acceptable to be picky over the first days... That's why I'm telling you shouldn't be crazy or fanatic, ever. Having said this, you will never see me ordering a burger or a big steak, or ribs or a fish plate for myself.

We have only commented on fear in the physical body so now let's look at the mental body.

It is clear that if you follow the advice regarding the physical body, it will have a psychosomatic effect on your mind and on the rest of the bodies. It is the first step to eliminate mental fear. Every day I have uncountable healthy thoughts, I am really healed. I have healed everything, all of my past and all of my future, and I am very comfortable living my present every single day, vibrating within me in states of lucidity.

So, if we are not afraid, why does our mind start to think without our consent? Because we didn't tame it completely, and taming takes time my friend.

The key with your mind is to stop and decide if we listen to it or not. That's the root for everything else to happen. After that, determine if you believe what your mind says or not; and finally, it will be activated consciously or subconsciously. **I know this is the problem everybody has because I was in that hamster wheel too.** In my past, I listened to my mind at all times, and I believed it. This was the biggest fail, because on top of that, I made those intrusive thoughts my own thoughts, as if I had created or generated them in a conscious way. I already told you the story of Sarita with her boyfriend… notice the hamster wheel inside where we all live, and no one telling us this secret about THE INTRUSIVE THOUGHTS. Every human being living a subconscious life… what a shame.

From here, it depends on your intelligence and your willpower and how you activate it. You have my support, but I mainly wish you start living a conscious and free life.

Let's go now with our emotional body and how to stop being afraid emotionally.

Think about everything I said before about jealousy, you must be conscious that it is them. You should know how to differentiate if it is serious or if they are laughing at you over nothing important. You really start to manage your emotional body properly when you start loving yourself for real. But you must believe this 100%…it is not enough just to read, say or know it. The key to empowering yourself in your emotional body is to believe it, learn how to live without fear and with trust.

For example, let´s look at how we start a serious relationship with a girl. We try to imitate the style of social programming based on the princess, prince charming and the castle. I insist that I really don't like this social engineering, I think there are different ways and options. So, we made a pact, we need to believe this pact, if not, it is worthless. So I insist again, in order to not be afraid in your emotional body you must be a master in knowing how to live ´overboard´ have faith and be a master in believing. If we succeed, when the MANTISES come to parasitize us with jealousy, they won't succeed. Remember that jealousy is a parasitism by mantises, that's why I insist in believing and living our human relationships to the maximum faith and trust. This is so we don´t let these beings feed on us and so we can eliminate them at once from this physical plane masterfully control our consciousness. If we do control our jealousy, mantises will stop feeding on us and will starve; the same goes with controlling our fears, our anger and aggressiveness…archons will stop feeding on us and will starve. This is when you start getting rid of ´bugs´ in the astral plane. They will starve to death or they will search for another victim, a weaker one. **Now that you are conscious about this war being waged in our face and that we can't see, we must spread the word of what's happening to us, what's happening on the astral plane, and** what's happening deep inside of us, in our microcosm. For people to find out about this war and this very magical knowledge to empower ourselves and live a freer life, ALL OF US need to detecting these intrusions and parasitism. Therefore, it is necessary that they read this book. I would appreciate it a lot, if you could take some time to leave the book and recommend it to people via Instagram, Amazon, Facebook, Gmail, WhatsApp, Telegram… in any way you can.

I sincerely thank you for taking that moment, to share this book or share the Amazon link with the people you know. I know that you did because we both know that this is very important. And I really hope that you start living a more conscious life like I do, without so much mental and emotional garbage. I feel so free and liberated from everything. I don't need anything from anyone. I can get around on my own and look after myself. If I have to ask for help, I have many people willing to help me, but I am not really one that asks for help, unless I am really struggling, I won't ask. If I am really struggling big time, then I will make the first move and ask for assistance.

We all have to fight this war, we all need each other. However, in order to wage this war, first we must know who our enemies are. It all starts because we are our own enemies, because they parasitize us through the pineal gland, and on top of that, we believe everything that they say through our manipulated little brains, activated with social engineering due to the education system and TV. There is still so more to teach and learn. Let's carry on.

Many people say "Uuuh, trust no one, or they will hurt you…"
Do you really think that I will live a life full of fear?
Third or fourth division people are completely lost in their own egos…completely unaware of their damage, their harm, how to live in the present with maximum lucidity. They are slave to intrusive feelings, parasitized with fear…
Mistrust and suspicion are low level fear; mistrust seems like it wouldn't be fear, but it is.

Here in Basque Country, my family always told me that things can be done in two different ways. One is with fear, doubt, insecurities and suspicion. The other one is with courage; we must be brave and face whatever comes; only trust and time will tell. I think it is for this reason that we 'basques' (people from the Basque Country) are different. Bravery is our thing; we are brave and we have big balls.

When someone breaks your trust and breaks you 100%, I recommend you pick up your things and leave without further ado, without making a fuss verbally, physically, mentally, or emotionally… If they break you, get your things and just go. Disappear, because they don't want you there, that's clear. Or maybe they really want and love you, but… technically **these people could be a slave of those beings and of their own subconsciousness.** This is one of humanity's biggest problems, I can still see a lot of 'puppet' people.

When we vibrate outside of ourselves, we are dumb, that'd the way it is.
Jealousy in particular is dangerous…it could perfectly well be that they just have a good friendship, nothing else. Besides, if we don't trust our partner in the least, we are dishonorable because we are breaking the pact. If there is a pact, there is a pact and we must fully go ahead with that, with everything.

Having reached this point, I sincerely prefer to live a life giving everything and trusting than living in fear and lost in paranoia. Remember that a human being is a creature of habit, so you can be a master in suffering jealousy or a master of trust. Each one of us, with time, will specialize in what he practices the most, be careful. The same happens with a mother that lectures her kids 7 days a week. On the 7th day, simply out of habit, she will look for anything just to reach the 7th lecture. **BE CAREFUL WITH SUBCONSCIOUS PROGRAMMING OUT OF HABIT**. Beware of epigenetics because you evolve inside yourself.

Considering how beautiful living true love is: he or she loves me, knowing that for real and living for it! I won't ever have the energy of jealousy in my energetic body, or of doubts or distrust; never. They intoxicate the energetic body and by psychosomatic effect, the rest of the bodies like heart and mind will become intoxicated. The spirit will be sad because you have a chance to live love in your present, but because you are weak, you will let yourself be intoxicated, you intoxicate yourself and you intoxicate the other people. I will never practice witchcraft inside of my body. I won´t give it power and focus, or the strength for the energies of doubt and mistrust inside of my energetic body. It would contaminate the 30 billion cells of my body; I would be dumb and also a toxic transmitter antenna of negativity. I have learned how to really shine; I am supernatural.

Moreover, I'm not going to give attention to the fear inside my energetic body, we must be more responsible. Emotional fear is the most difficult, because it activates the energetic body and attracts rot. When emotional fears are activated, your energetic body rots. It is here where you feel an infinity of unhealthy energetic sensations that you are not able to understand because you can't identify them. But after reading this, you will identify that an unhealthy rainfall of sensations happening inside can occur when you suffer from jealousy. Whether this is with or without a legitimite reason or not... or whether it is a conscious jealousy because someone is laughing in your face (being wronged), or a subconscious jealousy without a reason to be real but you still can't control it.

If you do listen to these jealous thoughts, and you believe them, this rainfall of energetic sensations, these intrusions and these manipulations are the power of mantises. Their power is mainly based on the fear of the emotional body, on our heart. If you believe these thoughts, their friends (the archons) will come to feed on your sadness, feeding on your energetic body. I think that you know exactly what I am talking about. I know that at some point you have been a victim of those spells and you didn't realize. You suffered it in a subconscious way, because you couldn't detect it, because no one has taught us how to identify these things, and it is one of the most important things in this life, to identify, RECOGNISE. (In Spanish the translation is RECONOCER, it can be read backwards and it reads the same). TO RECOGNISE is part of your light body, of your spirit. I really have faith in this book, in order for people to change, improve and evolve.

So, the most important thing of all is detection...how do you detect it? I'm asking you to be calm, because if you are new to this, at the beginning you will need some time to detect and realize it. If you have realized it and detected it; this is huge advantage in life. I'm sure that others are waiting for you to train and polish your inside more, to succeed in being supernatural and to be a freer human being without that many intrusions. If you really have willpower, the detection time will decrease and maybe these fears, doubts and suspicions will be detected before they are 'believed', so you can stop doing it and be more at peace. At a this stage you will get ahead and detect them when you are listening to them (not believing them). And later, you will detect them as soon as they begin in your mind and it won´t matter if it is in a mental, emotional or energetic manner. With time, these intrusions will stop getting produced. You can become a master and a magician of eliminating intrusions. Remember that this is the pattern that we follow:

1- WITHOUT OUR CONSENT SOMETHING BECOMES ACTIVATED IN OUR BEING
2- WE LISTEN TO IT CAREFULLY
3- WE BELIEVE EVERYTHING
4- WE ACTION IN A SUBCONSCIOUS MANNER

This whole book is of course important, but the part you are reading right now is the most important...I insist, WHEN you are going to action, try to make the click, like a wax on wax off kind of thing. I want you to be a magician in detecting this, and this really takes time.

People who are newer to this will take more time in realizing, maybe a day or two, or maybe weeks... But the key is realizing the intrusion suffered, and jealousy is a good example of this. If you keep up with the inner work, you will start realizing in a shorter time. Even you can realize in the 4th point of the pattern above and not take action in a subconscious way and say, "What's happening here? They are already manipulating me, getting me into trouble" then we can consider that an improvement. If you keep polishing your inside and working on your microcosm you will come to realize the intrusions on the 3rd point, when you are believing them, and you will say "Why should I believe this, distrust my partner and bring dishonor, breaking the pact that I made?". Effectively, if we keep polishing our inside we can even come to detect the intrusion at the 2nd point, when we are listening carefully to our mind which started thinking without our consent, when we are listening to our heart or when we are listening to all of these energies in our energetic body. If we don't surrender and we keep being vigilant and conscious, we could reach the day where we detect the intrusion right at the 1st point, exactly when some of the bodies start to think without our consent, activated on its own.

Working on our inside, on our microcosm, is changing our epigenetics, because we are moving from being subconscious slaves (that are guided through patterns), to conscious human beings that break patterns and are able to deprogram and reprogram themselves.

Living through this process, I promise, it is something magical and liberating in all senses.

I also have to say, that **there is a lack of female magicians**. This may be due to χ reason but you get your ego activated by lyonels and you end up actioning in a subconscious manner. I'm not saying this to cause offense, but I'm suggesting the process is more difficult for you, or social programming is harder on you. One thing I can see is that when we were kids, in the classroom, we used to say "he/she is such a girl" as an insult! If a boy spent the day with the girls, he was a wimp. Even playing football we used some of those 'insults'. Since the beginning of their lives, girls (not women), were never valued... Then you grow up, you become pretty, we run after you, and finally you get attention...maybe then your ego, or the Lyonel, gets activated... honestly... I don't know what is... **it is more difficult for you.**

A friend of mine, a rough one, says that it is because you have 200gr less of brain, I don't believe that this is the reason because I have seen men that don't look like they even have 1kg of brain. For example, a typcial gym guy with a mosquito brain that can only see the physical body, and the rest don´t exist.

They manipulate us so much from the energetic body and from our heart, be careful.

I love the example of jealousy, it is the clearest example to see how we vibrate outside of ourselves with energy lost on the outside, a drained energetic body. Another example is when a very strong relationship is broken. I remember the year 2020, I thought and vibrated outside of myself, far away, only concentrated on my ´soulmate´. I would be cleaning my house, and she would just come to my mind, my heart and my energetic body. We lived the most powerful love of our lives. Even today, she comes to me, mentally, emotionally and energetically, I can feel her, but I realize and I say "What am I doing vibrating outside if myself, with that melancholy energy?" and I stop it. I am conscious that this is an energetic drainage. So, in order to be a master of vibrating inside yourself, in states of lucidity in the present, first you have to be a master of detecting all these little things that take you out of your center.

In the end, **fear** is that, it makes you vibrate outside of yourself in an uncertain future full of **doubts**. It stresses you out and takes you out of your center. I hope that in the next few days you start to detect that you are vibrating on the outside and also that you may have the courage to return to your center and live your life.

Many people live a subconscious life, completely vibrating outside the whole day; it is sad but true. I hope this book reaches many people and that **we change the world to be a better place.**

At this point, as managers and masters of this information, there comes a time when the evil, fear and doubt that rot us, come to bore us. Here is where you start developing a taste for life and feeling comfortable. When you really live that "-Evil and that shit bore me".

The problem is when you meet someone who wastes their time with fear and evil. That person will bore you...this happens to me. It is true, **I get terribly bored with people full of fear, they are walking drainages.** Notice that, some people have become masters in vibrating on the outside and on top of that, vibrating in bad energies. People don't realize, but they are masters in witchcraft and dark arts in the energetic body. With what we know now about our little friends in other planes, this is because they parasitize you, drain your energy or even insert some etheric implants.

That's why it is so important to vibrate inside ourselves, in states of lucidity in the present, neither in the past nor in the future.

I'm tired of fear. It bores me.

When you are a kid, managing fear is harder.

Detecting mental and emotional fear is important. Because energetically, they drain us.

A very important thing is nutrition. If you eat a lot of meat, which is essentially dead cells that have suffered murder, death and fear, you will be that. If you consume the energy of fear, death and blood, that's the energy you will have on your inside and that you will be.

Notice the difference between eating a juicy mandarin, **living cells, full of sunlight, full of life.**

Therefore, when you love, you will love so much stronger, with more power, with more light. This love will be real, without doubts, without fears. This is something I really like, since I am a vegan, I love more and I love better. Whenever you eat, ask yourself which energy do you consume.

13 LIMITING PATTERN AND ARBORESCENT THINKING

´Limiting patterns´…that's a phrase I learned thanks to my friend Mel, from Masambala. In that eco-village, I remember that I said twice "but it´s just…" and she told me "That's a limiting pattern" …
For example, if I tell you to stop drinking coffee, and stop smoking, all of the excuses that you may say to not do it are known as a ´limiting pattern´.
This is even in spite of you knowing how bad coffee and smoking are for you. It is clear that a pattern is repeating itself. You must analyze if that pattern repeating inside you is conscious or subconscious. Effectively, the limiting pattern lies in the subconscious.
The funny part is that this is the same people that have trouble sleeping, stress or anxiety. In theory, a coffee is a bomb and you are having four cups a day. If on top of that you smoke so your lungs have less oxygen, I will give you the intelligence award.
Many people live a subconscious life and they don't even know it.
Many people live life as a slave to their automatic impulses and live without actioning or cutting out unhealthy addictions. Knowing how to cut something out or not give in is an art, action is an art.

ACTIONING BREAKS THE LIMITING PATTERN

People don't really like coffee; people like the mess of transgenic plants and additives that it has, but they don't even know it. However, then there are many people that know, but they don't care. They end up becoming masters of using a limiting pattern just like the person that spends all day insulting others, they become a master of insults.

You can detect a limiting pattern with the following phrases:
´But, I could, I should, it´s just, I will do it later, I will do it tomorrow and I don't ever do it…´
To keep oneself on a side, or to not action, can also be a limiting pattern depending on the situation which we will see further on.

The limiting pattern also exists when a programming exists. For example, there are some new age programs telling you that no one can touch your quartz or gems otherwise they will be contaminated by other people's energy. Let's think; if I touch your gems with all of my love, energy frequency and love vibration with wonder and gratitude because you let me see them… Do you really think that I will contaminate them? Please… there are so many weak people that allow themselves to be programmed so quickly and easily. Another example is that concept of connecting with the moon, vibrating on the outside; please, these are etheric contracts. Don't connect yourselves with the sun, or the moon, or the earth… Vibrate inside yourselves with states of lucidity in the present.

People lightly use their energetic body, without responsibility and with ignorance.

So that concept of not letting anyone touch your gems or shouting at people is a limiting pattern, it is limiting you and in a non-sensical way. Having said that, if you do let highly toxic people touch your gems, then yes, some of the energy can be transferred to the gems, but just some. I know this because it took me two years to fully fill a transparent quartz, so the energy is not transferred in just a second.

A limiting pattern is when you have a belief imposed via social programming or behavioral epigenetics or transgenerational epigenetics in a clan-like energetic level. It is a created pattern, a program, something that always repeats. For example, someone talks about geoengineering and you just laugh at it or ignore it. A few days after, someone talks about the same topic, and your response is the same. **Until you start listening and having empathy** for what is being said, you are not going to break that limiting pattern. Being in your comfort zone, from which you don't want to get out, you have a pattern created, and it is a limiting pattern. When we detect a limiting pattern, we should do some inner work of the microcosm. We should action, in order to activate arborescent thinking. This name is given because of a tree, and its branches that expand. Can you imagine a tree growing in your mind in all directions? That is the sensation of the arborescent thinking, an infinity of possibilities. It is curious how we are programmed so we can't see or we don't want to see certain uncomfortable truths.

A limiting pattern is an intrusive thought that doesn't let you move forward or progress, that doesn't let you see the truth.

For example, on an energetic level, you may think 'I can't get paid more than my parents do, because of an χ reason, so you surrender to a squalid job, with a squalid salary. This is a limiting pattern through transgenerational epigenetics to an energetic level. You created the idea in your mind that you can't be better than your previous generation...or your own parents created that idea in your mind...

Limiting patterns are all the beliefs that act as a break to our own evolution. Limiting patterns exist in your mind and are transmuted.
For example, one day, my friend Mel told me:
- **"Fuck, the same thing always happens to me, I'm tired of this, why can't I get out of this loop?"**

This is most likely due to a limiting pattern; you must focus and observe inside yourself, and in order to do so, you must have some level of mastery as an observer of your inside. That won't happen overnight, I mean, the fact that you are able to see further than what your eyes can see won't happen overnight. After observing, you must detect that limiting pattern in your inside in an either mental, emotional or energetic level; but for that, you must be a master of detection. And once you can detect it, and once you know what it is, what everything is about, you must transform it inside of you, transcend it inside of you and break the pattern. In other words, try to deactivate old brain neuronal circuits in order to activate new and better ones. Deprogram yourself and reprogram yourself.

Everything comes down to your subconscious.
Remember, without allowing it, people get activated subconsciously, and the worst thing we can do in such cases is to listen to it and believe what it is telling us as if it were an absolute truth.

I'm sure that we all have stood in front of the mirror regretting something we have done wrong…for example not being able to get out of a loop…
Now you know that this is due to the limiting patterns in our subconscious, I hope you can try to free yourself. It will all depend on either our cowardice or our courage to act in time.
Limiting patterns can also activate certain frustration, anguish or distress.

Giving a chance to new truths and new thoughts is arborescent thinking, we need this to break limiting patterns. The next time that someone tells you an uncomfortable truth, or something that really does not add up, give that person a chance and have **more empathy**.

14 THE "ENERGETIC PUNCH" DRAINAGES

We must consider that if we are too weak, too sensitive and we don't control our microcosm like "glass dolls", we will constantly be faced with drainages. I was also a glass doll...everything bothered me, everything made me feel down, and I was only 22 years old. I could never understand why. Back then I didn´t understand that you could be parasitized from other planes - mainly through your subconscious, with intrusive thoughts, through the pineal gland.

Years ago, in a telecommunications class, there was a classmate who couldn't get the binary system exercises right. I remember that I stood up, and said something like: -¨Dude! You still can't do it, we´ve been doing this for three weeks, come on!!´-

Let's look at that scenario from the energetic plane, you can see the lack of intelligence and control that I had. A classmate is struggling with an exercise, well that´s his problem, right? I was vibrating far away from myself, I was vibrating in my classmate and on top of that, vibrating in his problems...It is up to him, he has to work on it; it would have been better if I had remained silent, so he could have focused better. Anyway, a glass doll´s problem is that, it is always vibrating outside of itself and even in the problems of others. Is there anything less intelligent than this? Impossible. I always tell you, vibrate within yourselves, inside yourselves, and with a state of lucidity in the present. Don't vibrate outside, or in the past or the future...

After this introduction, let's study the drainages in our body. These drainages will always affect the energetic body, draining energy one way or another.

DRAINAGES IN THE PHYSICAL BODY:
Some examples of drainage of the physical body could be a nymphomaniac partner. Or, the typical guy that constantly taps you while talking, or the one that flicks you. Or the people that get way too close when talking to you, or get so close you can smell their breath. These **physically uncomfortable situations** can drain some energy from your energetic body.

DRAINAGES IN THE MENTAL BODY:
This can happen when you understand something, and someone close to you does not. It is difficult for them, and you have to explain it several times. This steals energy and time from your life. If they drain you in the mental field, it is because we are not as intelligent as we might think. We must know better, manage the situation better. Once you realize that you can control your mind, your life changes to a better and more conscious one.

DRAINAGES IN THE EMOTIONAL BODY:
This is where more energetic drainages occur, with romanticism, ego and love...
Criticism and REPROACHES, are emotional drainages and are draining your energetic body. People who

criticize are very draining people. THREATS such as "Oh, you will see when..."
Many times, in romantic relationships, when one party feels offended, lyonels are activated, the ego gets activated and says "now you will see, get ready for this...; I am going to make you feel as offended as I am, or even more". That is known as a toxic relationship. RIVALRY in this body results in a drainage. I find it so peculiar because making others feel bad is not in my behavioral code. If anyone wishes others misery, whatever it may be, even the tiniest misery, they have been parasitized by archons. Offended people are parasitized by lyonels. Sometimes we lose our temper and cause damage in an energetic way. By losing oursleves energetically, we generate those notorious energetic punches.

Once an energetic punch hits you, it can energetically hurt you for several days. There are people that back feed on them and can make them last for months or even years. The worst part, is that they become masters in back feeding on drainages, so when there is no drainage, they will try to create one out of habit.

I'm sure you remember something that has massively affected you in an energetic way. However, this is the first time you are recognizing what energetic punches are. These punches stay impregnated in your body, draining you. This is not physical or mental; it may be something emotional but mainly it is in your energy where you feel it. If you are a clone, you won't feel anything.

The truth is, if you try to control it from your mental body or emotional body, you will soon realize that you can't, and that the effect of the energetic punch still lies there. We are not properly trained in our energetic body. The system is not interested in teaching you that; they activate your body, and especially your eyes so you can see and desire things. They activate your mind, and especially your subconscious, but they don't teach you any of this in school, nothing about emotional intelligence, and much less about the energetic body. Having DEMANDS also can be energetic punches if good manners are lost. There will always be demands: subconscious demands (unhealthy ones) and conscious demands (healthy ones). Do you know that feeling, that thanks to you, your relationship is successful? But you are the one leading the way? Well, if we ´demand´, in a healthy way, that our partner should also make an effort, it is not a bad thing. The truth is that I have had some long-lasting relationships and I have seen how they clearly fought for me, and I fought for them. In other short-term relationships I saw how they didn't fight for me at all, so, in those cases, if I didn't feel fulfilled, I just left and disappeared.

I remember someone I met, she was at the hospital due to bad peritonitis. I have a very busy life and I don't keep a close eye on my phone. Some days passed and she called me asking if I was not going to visit a friend who had almost died. You can see this in the mental body or the emotional body, but let's see it from the energetic body because this was complete emotional blackmail. She was there, vibrating outside herself, vibrating in me, in the energy of blackmail, in the energy of demands and even in the energy of death, with the phrase "I almost died". These are high levels in witchcraft, energetically speaking. Yes, it's true that it was a tricky situation, but with those bad manners, it is converted into a situation of the famous Spanish Inquisition.

We must recognize all of these energies, because if you suffer from drainages, there are archons feeding on you. It is a very important thing to remember, THEY ARE DRAINING YOU.

Drainages occur because people are blocked. You can try to help, but you will end up being robbed of your time because realistically you will never be able to help blocked people; there is only one possibility and this is that they help themselves. I have tried to help a lot of people and the same pattern repeats itself over and over again. You end up wasting time, and often they even become your enemies. Unfortunately, we are driving in sixth gear and people are always in a rush. Each of us is a certain age, each of us has experiences, we all are different universes.

Often I say that when you close a black door, three white windows open in front of you. Almost everyone surrounding me right now are pretty brilliant. I don't have relationships with zombies anymore. Light is so important, loving yourself and being able to not consent and say "you are draining me". **Let's not be glass dolls complaining every second (ego),** let's not be masters of weakness. I recommend you to be a master in knowing how to cut drainages, and knowing how to cut them elegantly and tastefully, without attracting archons. In other words, with some temperance and self-control. A drainage is any situation that bogs you down.

15 TRANSMUTATION TECHNIQUES

My two favorite transmutation techniques are smiling and breathing. I wanted to dedicate a chapter to them because they really help us to vibrate within ourselves, within states of lucidity in the present. I want you to stick some notes around your house, at work, in your car etc with these two words:

SMILE
BREATHE

I practice a lot of smiling and conscious breathing.
Do the following exercise. Put the book down. Stand up and focus seriously, stay there in serenity, ANALIZE THE ENERGY OF SERIOUSNESS (you will see that it is pretty conscious, it is not good or bad, it doesn't rise or lower your frequencies, it is a pretty good energy for studying). Now, indulge yourself with a sincere smile, allow that smile to get bigger and bigger. You will feel how your whole energetic body activates by itself. In fact, this is a rule to practice Chi-kun or Qi-Gong: to smile. Another rule is conscious breathing. With the hustle and bustle of daily life and the constant rush, we even eat quickly and subconsciously. This means our breathing has also been programmed like this, in a hurry. We don't even focus on breathing anymore, sad but true. We are always living outside, and we must learn to live within ourselves, inside ourselves; we must feel ourselves again, we must recognize ourselves again, we must love ourselves again.
Imagine your connection to the five bodies as if it were a marriage. I am sure that you would have married your mind and your heart, and maybe your physical body. But if this were a marriage, your energetic body would be abandoned just like your spiritual body. We must go back to loving ourselves again in all the senses and be conscious of our five bodies. We should try to detach a little bit more from our mind and heart, who have always been holding the reins for so long. We have been subconscious slaves to them. But now we are in charge.
A SMILE is key to opening our energetic knots. If at any time you feel a presence, or as if someone is watching you, smile. I remember emperor Marcus Aurelius in the film *Gladiator* said: "Death smiles at us all, all a man can do is smile back."
MAGICIAN BREATHING
It is difficult to explain, so it is better for you to hear it so you don't doubt it. Breathe in, filling your lungs, a lot, but not to the maximum, and expel the air with an AAAAAAHHHH sound. Release the air calmly but in a magical way, almost as if it were a pulmonary orgasm. You have to release the air with total serenity, total relax and total pleasure.
Conscious breathing doesn't age; in fact, if you forget to breathe, you will age faster.
Remember that we have forgotten a lot about our bodies...they are sad because we don't give them attention...
When your body is full of oxygen many things happen, you have more aura, your physical body can resist more. It regenerates itself and it heals you faster. In addition, your mind will withstand problems

and find solutions way faster, and probably that solution will be more effective. Being full of oxygen is a power that goes unnoticed. Blood flows better, which is better for our heart. Conscious breathing changes your life.

I will leave this blank page if you want to write any insights, learnings or findings that caught your attention:

16 THE AVATAR

I hope you are practicing the smile and the conscious breathing, cultivating your energetic body in all respects. Feel powerful, with your aura activated, and above all, feel the five bodies you have and don't let any of them become abandoned or 'orphan-like' which is what we have been doing up to now.

In this chapter, I was to explain another technique: the one of keeping quiet, it is called the observer technique. To be honest, I used to never shut up, and I have learned to leave an argument when I want to go unnoticed or to be invisible. Before, I explained the silly example of being in class, vibrating in a classmate who was struggling with a binary system exercise. Imagine if, in that moment, instead of behaving as I had, I had just kept quiet. If I had practiced the observer technique, I would have seen my mind full of intrusive thoughts complaining, vibrating outside of myself in the energy of concern. I would have been conscious of all the automatisms inside my microcosm. It was my dumb ego that I will never understand, but through social engineering, they programmed it and activated it to high levels. However, I have already deprogrammed myself of the "not keeping quiet" program.

This technique was taught to me by Extremi6 psychedelic warrior. And the truth is that when you practice it, you realize many things. I remember him telling me: "Sometimes I wonder, why would I say something if they are not going to listen? I'm not wasting energy; I'll just vibrate inside myself in states of lucidity. Fine. I'll pass". He's right, often it is like this. I'm sure it has happened to you at some point, that you spoke and then thought: I shouldn't have said anything. This is a very odd technique.
After some time, I realized that this is an "energy-saving mode" technique, and keeps drainages minimized, meaning you avoid arguing about small things by practicing to stay silent. Actually, if you argue over silly things, you are silly or dumb, as simple as that. Sometimes I realized I was arguing over a stupid thing, and that there is something about that in social engineering, as if we have the 'arguing mode' activated. Be careful, because there are people who are masters in arguing and doing so several times a day; watch out for who you invest your time in, because you will become a master in that. Watch out for arguments, the root (cause) and the percentage % with which you contributed in starting them.

One day you will wake up and think: today I will practice keeping silent; and I'm telling you that you'll end up developing a taste for that. Furthermore, if you do it right and keep quiet, you will see all the automatisms in your body wanting to trigger you to talk or jump in, both with intrusive thoughts and intrusive energies. Besides the energy-saving mode (not talking to who does not listen to you), in the observer technique and remaining silent, you can see many things you couldn't see before because we were part of the subconscious drama of the theatrical play. Often, we are too attached to the body and we are slaves to the impulses of our avatar. We are here to separate ourselves a little from our avatar, because we are not a biological suit, we are much more than that; although many people live locked inside their avatar without seeing the energetic body, which is the most important, it is where they drain us, and we don't realize.

Energy-saving mode: I don't talk if I don't have anything to say. Contribute or depart.

I don't try to prove myself or anything to anybody, unless they want to learn and purposely ask me to. The key to succeeding in the observer technique is not to be in the center of the bullring (or the amphitheater, if you will), but be out of it, observing and watching what is happening from the stands. This will be difficult for the rookies that still think they are their avatar; due to subconscious impulses, they are always in the center of the bullring, in the amphitheater arena. However, now we are talking about being out of it, in the barrier, from the stands.

We must practice the situations we live in, we should try to be a little bit out of the ´issue´, not the victimized main character and acting impulsively under the ruling of our subconscious. Practice remaining silent and stop trying to be the protagonist of everything that happens. This is just acting subconsciously and generating a theatrical play. It is difficult at the beginning, but it can be achieved. People with too much ego will always be victims of their life situations, or will always act like the main character of the subconscious play. I encourage you to practice remaining silent and observing in order to see how the mind, the heart and your energy start functioning without your consent to trigger it. Don't react - remember that in this technique, we are in the stands and not in the arena, don't react. If you can reach this point you will understand that you were in such a prison, full of intrusions. In addition, you will notice the mental, emotional and energetic impulses which made you live a whole life of slavery, thinking that you were free. At the moment where you notice that prison and the deception inside of you, don't suffer for all the subconscious life that you are living, just rejoice, because from now on, you can live a more conscious life, detecting intrusive thoughts, intrusive feelings and intrusive energies. If you take this book seriously in your real life, you can become a great master in all of these things and live a freer and more relaxed life, without so much mental or emotional garbage. Knowing how to recognize errors and identify those impulses that "force" us and trigger us to act is key.

The observer technique, helps us to see all those automatisms happening inside of us, automatisms that have gone unnoticed and we didn't spot them before. I insist, for the rookies; wake up one day and say: today I will practice the observer technique and remain silent; whatever happens, don't jump into the bullring and stay in the stands please!

This technique is a double-edged sword; for starters it is great because you realize a lot of things, but there is a trap - if we are always in observer mode, we don't take action, and if we don't take action, we are just "filler" people...second or third division people. What we can learn from this technique is to act consciously, and not from impulse, like before.

So now you are conscious about what's happening inside of you and what's happening outside of you, but if we overuse this technique, we stop acting, and that's a mistake. I always say, don't fall into fanaticisms about anything or anybody. Limits and extremes are always bad, we need balance here. What we need to do is cease that subconscious acting, but without being a slave to impulse or ego. We need more consciousness in this world, please.

I insist, when we are in ´observer mode´, without taking action and simply watching everything from the stands, the limiting pattern can be activated because we are doing nothing. The observer technique is great at the beginning, for novices, so they don't react, because they are addicted to reacting. Rookies are addicted to being in the center of the arena subconsciously because they can't detect those intrusive impulses and by trying this technique they will be more conscious. We must use these techniques if we use them consciously, and not the other way round, otherwise the techniques will end up using us.

For example, I used to argue with my father constantly about everything, absolutely EVERYTHING. One day, this technique came to me, so one day when we were arguing, he started to trigger me by reproaching things, and I realized…he was mentally attacking me, I was emotionally suffering because he is my father there were two very strong impulses mixing together. I practiced the observer technique; I didn't subconsciously jump into the arena, but instead just kept listening, putting aside all the mental garbage and emotional scourge that this conversation was causing me. This was the first time I noticed all the mental, emotional and energetic chaos that I had been suffering. I went to my bedroom to process everything that had happened during the conversation. It was a victory for my consciousness; I marveled because we didn't argue; it was the first time we didn't end up shouting at each other. It was also the first time that I was aware of the subconscious and all of these mental, emotional, and energetic impulses. It was one of the first times I realized how much garbage we have inside that doesn't really let us live, and I could see it by practicing the observer technique.

If I had felt offended, or had listened to an intrusive thought, intrusive emotion or intrusive energy, and believed it… I would have reacted as usually would have, and we would have had a big fight. In this level I felt so "evolved", but I am the same as you, don't think that I am better than you, I just have more information and I act as a wise man by practicing what I know. However, I'm telling you that at this point, I can get it right first time and detect mental impulses or intrusive thoughts; I don't even let them complete the process. What I should practice more is controlling my emotional impulses or intrusive feelings, because I am very sensitive and that involves a lot of energy. When the heart is used, it's harder, but I´m telling you that we can become masters on an emotional and energetic level. I am on this path, and there are battles every day.

The truth is that, the first time that I did the ´observer technique´ with my father, I was surprised about all the garbage that we have inside us and everything I had to do internally to not have the same result as before…shouting at each other, with archons draining us.

Remember that this is "energy saving mode", meaning not to argue over small things. I remember that I was in full consciousness, watching how my body behaved while in observer mode, knowing that I should not act under those subconscious intrusive impulses. My mind really wanted to confront my father in the arena. This was probably out of habit, like my mind was missing some beef with my father, but I didn't give in to it; a tamed mind is better. After that, I recall that when he attacked me, my emotional body became activated subconsciously, from the outside. I hadn´t granted permission, and therefore felt attacked; I felt my ego vibrating without my consent for the first time.

So I told to myself and all those lyonels inside of me, to 'shut up' because we were practicing the observer technique and in energy saver mode.

When my father was done saying everything he had to say and saw that I wasn't going to argue, he was puzzled and confused, perhaps wondering why we were not arguing as usual...

After that I talked to him about non-negative things, like the veggie garden, the market, etc. It was the first time we had had a healthy conversation in such a long time. I was 29 and already on the path of detaching myself from the avatar, separating myself from the mental scourge, from the mental garbage and from the energetic, intrusive impulses. That's why I decided to write this book, because I've been practicing controlling my consciousness for some years.

But I insist, do not fanaticize, I know that this information is very powerful, but do not fanaticize. We must not go crazy even though it is heavy topic.

That's why this chapter is called 'The avatar' - because **you are not your avatar**. Remember the film Avatar, when the guy in a wheelchair enters the body of that blue native? He switches avatars, but he retains his etheric body and his light body. In other words, he keeps his soul and spirit. So, let me remind you that you are not your avatar, you are not your mind, and you are not your heart. Those are two tools that should be at your disposal, and it seems that everybody is a slave to their mind and heart. They don't recognize themselves; they don't recognize their soul or their spirit. Honestly, I lived for so many years enslaved by my mind, and even more by my heart.

Now you are more conscious about what we call the Matrix. There are many kinds of Matrix such as the inner Matrix and outer Matrix, and inside each of those there are more kinds.

We already talked about the gardener, who I despised due to imposed social programming. However, when this observer technique came to me, about not reacting, about doing nothing and watching how so many automatisms get triggered inside you without you even being conscious of it, I finally understood everything that I had been reading about neuroscience, psychology, and epigenetics over the past few years. Imagine I take action, and I throw a stone at him or any other possible scenario...these are subconscious actions. Now, as a consious thinker I am prepared and wish him a nice day. Notice how much the story changes when you leave your avatar and get away from the scourge, from this biological suit called "the body".

You have your physical body that you can see. Information enters through it provoking the first subconscious actions. This information is processed automatically in our brain, without our consent, in combination with our heart, which is in control of our feelings. Some energies will be generated that will more or less fool you, according to your level. However, energy is the most challenging aspect to understand, to identify, to detect, to associate, etc because we never practice controlling our energetic body.

I wanted you to see the whole process, due to this enigma, a response is generated in our being subconsciously. It is here where the sheeple will be a slave of this enigma, and it is here where the ´awoken´ will decide what to do. They will decide if to act subconsciously or to use their consciousness; in other words, choose between acting in the heat of the moment or to breathe, smile, relax and control the reaction consciously. I lived enslaved by my mental impulses for about 26 years and also by my emotional and energetic impulses. But no more. I am no longer a slave to the enigma that happens inside of us. I have a new life.

The theory of the observer technique ends here, but let's go a little bit further.
You are not just your bodies.
You are both a spirit and a soul trapped in a biological body with a mind and a heart.
You are not an avatar, so wake up. YOU ARE NOT AN AVATAR.
You have already spent your whole life living as if you were an avatar...
When will you wake up and realise that you are much more than that?
I am a soul and a spirit too.
Don´t be an energetic body that is drained by other beings from other planes completely unaware.
They fooled us with the avatar, heart, and mind. Half the story has never been told to us, my friends...
We also have the theory that everything is a hologram, that our life is just a dream within a dream, or that we could be in a computer system like in the Matrix movies. There is an infinity of possibilities, arborescent thinking, and the notion that everything can be true. Nevertheless, if we are inside of the Matrix, we must detect the possible Matrix inside of this Matrix, (at least so that they don't make us out to be such fools).
Practicing detachment from our avatar in this physical plane, is the first step towards astral travel. Being in a daily routine, knowing that we are not the avatar, and detaching ourselves is key. Try not to totally despise your avatar either, but just realise, you are not it. They have deceived us. It is like a race course, are you the driver or are you the car? The car is your avatar, and the driver is you. We believe that spirit could not be part of the Matrix, but the avatar (the body), certainly is.

For example, when you go out running or jogging, and your biological body starts to sweat and tells you "I am tired" - you are not really tired, it is not really you who is sweating. It's the avatar that´s tired and sweating. If your mind believes it and if your heart feels it, you have a subconscious problem. Actually, your soul and your spirit don't have the ability to get tired; that is a result of the physical body...of the Matrix.
Some time ago, I remember at Kyokushinkai training, they made me reach my limits, so I started mindful breathing. When you detach yourself a bit from your avatar, by breathing, it is like your seventh sense gets activated. I stopped feeling dizzy, I stopped feeling tired, and started to feel like my body started to seem more like my limitless spirit. **Sometimes when you break your limits, you realize all the power you have.**

So, to go further, and reinforce the observer technique, let's look closer at the avatar and try to differentiate the biological body from the spiritual body. Over the day, you will repeat to yourself the following sentence: ´This is not me, this is my avatar.´

Simultaneously by discerning the avatar, and disposing of the biological suit, we need to see that we are also a spirit, a light body, that has everything. It is complete by default, and as standard, it is eternal; and this is how you should feel. Do this exercise several times a day, it will help you; because the more that you can differentiate between the the biological body and the spiritual body, the better. By doing this, you are also separating yourself a little bit from your heart and mind, and also reminds you that these are also not you. If you do this several times a day, the next time that your mind speaks without your consent, you will most surely catch it faster, improving your reaction and speed. When your heart next speaks, offended, without your consent, you will probably notice it faster. As mentioned before, this is also the initiation for astral projection or astral travel.

You are not you, I am not me, oh no, this is not me, this is my avatar, you are not you. You will notice this when you practice the observer technique, seeing the whole theatrical play of the scriptwriter, who sometimes almost deserves an applause. Plus, it makes you think that you can make decisions, which some of us know is not like that. We believe that it is all scripted and that's why we have déjà-vu; essentially life is a dream within a dream. This goes back to the infinity of possibilities and arborescent thinking.

To live better and calmer, we should get out of the subconscious prison, either on a mental level or an emotional level, and break the schemes of our Matrix prison.

For example, you are at work one day, quite stressed; if you realize that the stressed one is the avatar and not you, you will laugh about it and understand it.

I find it funny when people are arguing, because I see them locked in their mental prisons, and I would like to tell them that they are not their avatar. The observer theory is pretty good, but it does not completely embrace the avatar nor does it completely embrace the spirit. The practice of the constant unfolding in this physical plane can be ´suffered´ by both parties, either by the avatar or by the spirit; that's why it is such a critical practice. The more connected you are to your spirit, and knowledgable you are about separating your bodies, or at least differentiating them, the easier it will be and the better you will become in detecting intrusions. We have been our avatar's slaves for so long, let's detach a bit from them.

For example, we are in the kitchen doing whatever, and the phone and the doorbell ring at the same time. Many people get nervous as a slave to their avatar. The acoustic signals trigger the mental subconscious to be in a rush and answer... this is nonsense. Relax, please, this is the Matrix talking, nothing will happen...it's okay. We must start living without being in a rush, because that rush makes you be a slave of the subconscious. Uninstall the programs to rush. Rush is stressful (and it makes you age), and many people practice it on a daily basis without being conscious that they are authentic masters of living in a rush, or in other words, living enslaved by their avatar...

17 THE MASTER OF TIME

I do hope you are practicing smiling every day, as well as conscious breathing and magician breathing. Normally, after 21 days of practicing these, if you forget, it will be your own brain who reminds you to give him wellness and more oxygen, because he likes it. It becomes a habit. Conscious breathing is something they blatantly stole from us through social programming, and encouraging us to always be in a rush.

Let´s talk about numbers. Numbers were created in Babylon, and actually they are witchcraft (SUMERIA). In my opinion, they are spells made to make us age. That's why they program us so much and force over and over again to write the date: day, number, month and year. Time is, for me, a program that they have forced us to install in ourselves since we were kids. They have put a lot of effort into social programming and social engineering. At primary and secondary school it was mandatory to write the date, every, single, day…what a cheek! I often ask myself: how would a human being be without the manipulation-statement that time exists? How would a human being be without a track of time? He could be more eternal, with more durable, when you compare it to supposed "time". Being lost in time also makes you age; if you are obsessed with the date and time, you have fallen into their trap. **You realize this with their insistence and obligation** to install in us the program of time. It is a very hard-wired program that we all have deeply installed. In order to uninstall it we must practice the *"I-don't-sweat-it"-ation*, the "I don't care" (from now on, referred as SWEATATION). Which month are we in?, I don't sweat it; What day is today? I don't sweat it, What time is it?, I don't sweat it. **We should stop celebrating times and start celebrating this day and everyday.**

For me, birthdays are a form of witchcraft to make you age. I will celebrate when I see a bright blue sky, with natural, pompous 3D clouds every day.

July, August, September… Which month is September? Yes, the ninth month. So why does it start with sept? Where does that come from? Doesn't sept come from a root meaning seventh or seven? So then, is it the 7th month?... Do you realize now that there is manipulation out there? Or is it still difficult for you to believe? Could it be that you may have a limiting pattern that starts to break forcibly due to so much information and cognitive dissonance?

I am telling you that this is witchcraft at the highest level. They have put a spell on you about time…but there are giveaways! Shall we go on?

October, month 10… but it is really the 8th, oct, octagon…
November, month 11… but it is really the 9th – nov…
December, month 12… but it is really the 10th…
I hope you see the psychopathy of this spell and this poorly made program. Actually, we shouldn't have any track of time, and if we are guided by a calendar, it shoud be the lunar calendar. But I vote for not following any type of calendar or rule. **More freedom, more freedom.**

Being a master of time is based on if you practise it each day. People that laugh a lot during their day, they are masters in laughing. If a mother goes off at her children seven times a day, with time that mother will become a master in arguing seven times a day. If one day she argues six times, only out of habit she will by all means seek for arguement number 7. We must check the programs that we use, how many times a day we use them, and decide what to become masters in. We are masters in what we say, what we do, what we hear and what we see. For instance, if you are a master in watching TV, (which only tells you lies), in the long run you will be a master in hearing and seeing lies. If all of your relationships have been toxic, you are a master in being in toxic relationships; watch out as this affects your life.

18 THE POWERFULL BEAR

Activate the powerful bear. You do this when you have already been a master in detecting intrusions for some time, and you have a certain amount ´piloting´ or flight hours (experience) in conscious matters. For example, if you have been practicing conscious breathing and smiling for a while now. It is activated with the sweatation "I don't sweat it"-ation attitude towards the situation and being above the drama.

I learned the following saying from my friend Peru, who will translate this book into English. I really love this saying because it is sounds really good in a ´punk´ kind of way:

SWEATATION AT THE SITUATION
SWEATATION TO FACE THE SITUATION
SWEATATION IN FRONT OF THE SITUATION

So think to yourself: ´So, this happened… Yeah… I don't sweat it.´
It is true, that if we overuse this saying, we would verge on sheeple behaviour. However, if we are conscious about what we are training, it's okay.
When facing a serious problem, we have to activate the sweatation, the "I don't sweat it", "I don't care." That is not you, you are not the avatar, try to move away a little from your mental garbage and your emotional scourge. When it's been a while that you have been practising the concept that you are not your avatar, and you can differentiate pretty well the avatar from the spirit, you can practice sweatation in front of a situation.
The truth is, I've been practising sweatation my whole life, but now more than ever.

Actually, since I dug deeper into neuroscience and I started viewing matters consciously and subconsciously, the ´war´ in my life has decreased considerably. I don't have such arguments and don't get upset like before. Instead, I close the door on them, so I don't feed my ego. However, I have felt more attacks from the outside from parasitized people around me, and they attack me.

The next sentence is from Bandolera, and if you practice it, you will notice the emotional degree ego parasitism can reach: **BE ABOVE THE DRAMA.**
Impactful. You should write both phrases on post it notes and hang them around the house, the car, and at work. This way, you are actively trying to dispose of intrusions and egos. ´Be above the drama´, that is impactful. However, for people that eat a lot of meat, it is almost impossible for them to let go of their ego.

SWEATATION IN FRONT OF THE SITUATION, AND BEING ABOVE THE DRAMA ACTIVATE THE POWERFUL BEAR

This is a mastery only a few can reach. But mainly, the key is not to practice it just once, but to practice it constantly and continuously.

By the way, if you hang some post it notes in your house, and you and your partner are having an argument, if they see these papers, it´s likely they will stop arguing and their egos will be extinguished. It is important not to have wars, it is important not to have fears, and to be able to become the powerful bear.

When you have been practicing the powerful bear for a while and you reach a certain degree of confidence, then you can hack the Matrix. To do so, you can't be in low frequencies at any time. Then, you can activate **the path of the magician**; it is like a **supreme confidence, knowing that at the end of the path, a good solution awaits you.** This confidence, knowing it and believing it, is as if some gears in the quantum field are starting to move to find a decent solution to your problems. But be careful, this is only made within ourselves, and this is not us asking an external being, like Saint Pirulo or any other. **The path of the magician is an art, able to flip and turn the tables of your absolute evil and leave it better...**but you have to be trusting and in powerful bear mode.

19 DETECTING HEALTHY PEOPLE AND TOXIC PEOPLE

First, the toxic people:

Let's look at the best tips and tricks to recognize toxic or parasitized people:

- Changes and new truths bother them
- They can offend anyone without trembling and feel they are above you
- They don't usually or never give in, or compromise, they are stubborn
- They can't be alone or in silence
- **They shout, get enraged, they practice an aggressive wrath**
- They have the sickness of fear or doubt
- Fear and doubt make them manipulative, arrogant and insistent
- They can use emotional and mental blackmail when asking for help S.O.S.
- They can attack you for getting offended over silly things
-They will laugh at and stomp on your sacrifices or your achievements, they won't value them
- They are usually stressful and stress you out
- They tend to seek confrontation and rivalry
- VICTIMISTS, it's always them who suffer, the rest of us doesn't count, they can't see us
- THEY LIE, even with half-truths, **they hide the full truth**
- It is difficult for them to accept they were wrong, and they blatantly demand to be forgiven
- THEY BREAK PROMISES, they are from the broken word clan
- They give the sensation of stagnant relationship, they don't progress, they slow you down
- They are slaves of mental scourge and emotional garbage
- **They don't realise or don't want to realise that they live in a parallel world**
- They are able to inject fear in you, DISHONOUR, doubts, mandates, doubts, anger, terror...

Now, the healthy people:

Let's look at the best tips and tricks to recognize non-parasitized, healthy people:

- They practice honour, respect, patience, temperance and empathy
- They can sacrifice themselves
- They contribute to other's success and they are happy for other's success
- They *nurture* above all
- They will never attack you
- They will never act out of revenge
- They are grateful
- They dislike the sheeple
- THEY CAN SEE THEIR MISTAKES AND IMPROVE QUICKLY
- They are able to handle hard and heavy information
- They feel protected, infinite, and they believe it
- They don't need to parasitize anything or anyone
- They are experts in easily detecting imbalances
- They work on their inner self, their microcosm, they carry the responsibility of their life **without external help**
- **They have the habit of commitment and giving one's all**
- They practice union and freedom
- Their base is compassion and comprehension

20 ¿WHY DO PEOPLE NOT UNDERSTAND EACH OTHER?

Remember that everything is energy, frequency and vibration.
If you act as I do, feeding yourself with living cells, on a raw, frugivorous, vegan diet, a diet based on hydrants...rest assured that people that feed on dead cells won't be at the same height as your frequencies. You will carry the energy of life inside you, and they will carry the energy of death. Rest assured that the message from emitter to receiver will always have issues between two energies that are so different.

Check the previous page, people who nurture and people who under-nurture.
We must be conscious that there are some people we can't wake up.
We must detect the Smith agent in other people.
When you go out, you see eyes, a nose and a mouth on other people...and that's why we think that we are all equal, that we are all human beings. I have often thought that there are many races of eyes, noses and mouths, of course, as there are many races amongst human beings. However, not in the way you think. We have the awoken ones and the "impossible to awaken" ones.
Amongst the awoken ones, there are the *very* informed ones and the informed ones.
The majority of informed ones, still don´t reach subjects like neuroscience, psychology and epigenetics. That is to say, the majority of the informed ones are still asleep. And amongst the super informed ones, the best ones, a certain percentage is still subconscious and the other percentage is conscious. That's why I created this book, to turn the tables.

Honestly, I am teaching courses on this for free, and I can see how my life has been dynamited from other planes. Every time that I awaken someone, I have problems. I know it is them, because something surreal happens to me. Every time that something surreal happens to you, it is a glitch in the Matrix, it is them from other planes kicking up a fuss. They may use the people closest to you, parasitize them and turn them against you, or even more surreal things. However, every time something happens to you and leaves you in shock, I'm telling you it is them. They see that you are on the right track in life, so they think: - We will slow this one down - and that's how it all works. Every single time that I wake someone up, 3 to 6 days after, they cause a ´mess´, it's actually mathematic.
We often won't understand others, or they won't understand us, mainly because they are parasitized. And of course, they must be parasitized because they carry the energy of death by feeding on dead cells. It is not always like this, but it's true that parasitism happens more easily if you eat blood.

We must stop seeing eyes, noses and mouths. This is my way of saying "don't see the avatar", you must be able to see beyond that.
My opinion is that we all have the same spirit, but some of us have a more naked spirit than others, depending of the number of flight hours you have done on your inner work. If you have separated from the mental scourge and the emotional scourge, you will probably act more spiritually than under the

impulses of an offended heart or a subconscious brain.

What I'm saying is that we all have the capability, because if you close your eyes, and search inside yourself, starting on the solar plexus...and if you recognize yourself, if you feel yourself, it means that eternal energy is inside of you. That thing that you feel inside of you, is the same that I feel inside of me. That's why I advocate that we all have that light inside of us, that doesn't need anything, it has everything, it is complete and eternal.

The sprit has potency, and has a character, a temper, and sometimes it comes out and there is no one can overcome it. Don't confuse it with the subconscious or with archontic attacks...I insist, do not confuse or mistake it for the subconscious.

If you have a naked spirit, uncovered, if we consider frequency, you will be in an ideal spot. When you are here, you may find that you are able to really get along with people and understand each other, or you may find you don't get along at all with them and not understand a thing.

YOU CAN ONLY DELIVER YOUR MESSAGE TO THOSE WHO VIBRATE IN THE SAME FREQUENCY AS YOU

SOME PEOPLE SIMPLY CAN'T HEAR YOU, EVERYTHING IS A MATTER OF ENERGY FREQUENCY AND VIBRATION

That's why, if you have a naked spirit, you will be able to understand other people who are also in that advanced phase; you will get along with people who don't have a mental scourge or emotional garbage. Once you have reached this point, the reward is high as it is especially based on DO NOT MISTREAT and do not mistreat me.

If I don't consume poisons like sugar, coffee and blood, I can't get along or understand people who are addicted to sugar or coffee or blood. Moreover, they will probably argue with me and get stressed in a conversation or they may act upon something I say or do.

Remember to breathe consciously and always smile, we are made of sterner stuff.

Moreover, every one of us has a different soul. That's why we are so different, because we all have different souls. Depending on our experiences and depending on how much social programming has affected you, you will be one way or another. It also depends on the contact that you have had in your life with your spirit, because there are people who have never touched it and have not even realized that this light body existed. You can see it when, in a very dark situation, you shed a lot of powerful light – for example when there were four guys fighting against one at recess and I went to stop it as a powerful bear.

Light body – spirit – eternal, with potency and character, it has everything and does not need anything

Etheric body – soul – mind, heart and energy, our way of being

Physical body – biological suit – the car

These are the three bodies according to Eduardo Coletto.
For example, I am a lot like an eagle, very libertarian, I enjoy freedom, and anyone that stops that I won´t get on well with. Eagles like flying free, so I won´t get on with anyone that imprisons me with motivations of self-interest. I am also a horse, quite rough, quite fast and outgoing, so I don't get along with people like snails - slow people who slow me down. I am also a wolf, we have a saying in Spanish that literally translates to "see the wolf's ears", which means "to see the storm clouds coming", which is very characteristic of my being. For example, during that recess when there were four guys against one and I went to stop the fuss…I stood there looking at the others, shouting at them to ask if they were just going to stand there doing nothing. This wolf that dares to stop injustices is a characteristic of mine, with no fear, no matter how many guys there are to confront.

THE TIGER AND THE LION MAY BE STRONGER,
<u>BUT THE WOLF DOES NOT WORK FOR THE CIRCUS</u>

I also don't care about gossip or sensationalism; I always have been an advocate for anti-bullying. When I have had problems with someone, I have always gone 1 on 1. I never called more people to help me, or created a gang, or made any conspiracy to provoke and turn a group of people against one person. This is actually something that happened to me recently…a bunch of "acquaintances" turned against me and are making my life a bit more complicated.

But seriously, creating a conspiracy against a single person or turning a group of people against one person is not ok…I'm not into that. I think it is absurd, and even cowardly, not to mention an absolute dishonor. I actually prefer it the other way around: me against a few others. Needing other people to solve your problems is a pretty childish attitude, this means you believe that just yourself is not enough or you have a severe inferiority complex. These "acquaintances" are simply slaves of the reptiles, focused on attacking me, they do not have consciousness and they are ceasing to live their own life. They don't live their life, they live mine, they live in me. Notice how energetically unwise this is. They are vibrating outside of themselves, on top of that they are vibrating in me, with the energy of hate, of resentment, of distress, of discomfort… This is the epitome of unhealthy, witchcraft energy they are imposing on me. The saddest thing of all, is that they are not living their own life, they are not living in their present.
It is key to know that you are not parasitized, that you are vibrating inside yourself, in states of lucidity and in the present, not in the past or the future. If you add "being above the drama" to this,

and the "sweatation in front of the situation" you will become the powerful bear, lucid and moving forward (progressing), no matter what comes your way. Add to this "smiling and conscious breathing", and you will be following my rhythm.

Due to one reason or another, I see many people being a slave of their own emotional scourge, their ego...
I have been talking to several friends and we still don't know a single woman who has moved completely away from her emotional garbage. For one reason or another, they always end up being parasitized by lyonels, digging into their ego. **Let's see how Agent Smith of the Matrix takes control of the woman in red.** I don't want to be chauvinistic, but I do believe that women have a pretty serious problem with the ego of lyonels. I already gave you a note of warning, which you know already. Now take a look at your life, your day-to-day, be honest with yourself and analyze if this is not the case. I don't know why, it could be due to social programming that has activated your ego so much. I wish to remind you of some sayings from my mother:

ABUNDANCE KNOWS HOW TO BECOME DETACHED IN ORDER TO GIVE

YOU ONLY DEFEAT DARKNESS IN ONE WAY, WITH MORE LIGHT

I have been training for some years now, so if I get hurt nothing happens, it's fine. I don't start wars, but what I can do is to get out of those situations. I have been practicing for some time actually, because I am a little fed up with people wasting my time and being mistreated. So, since I had already counted several surrealist humiliations, I simply left. Bye. It's strange that, for some reason or other, other people don´t recognise these humiliations or they don´t want to see them. Therefore, if he or she does not want to see their mistakes, improve, and not mistreat, something's wrong.
I am talking about surreal humiliations such as being blatantly unfaithful in your face and with arrogance. Or someone recklessly driving, with the intention of injecting fear and terror into you, or the Lyonel attitude of "I am the commander and you are a nobody".

I think it is pretty difficult to differentiate what is surreal from what is not. This is mainly, because you end up wondering time and time again, if what's happening to you is real or not...
So, when someone plays several of these tricks on me, I just disappear and leave; I don't fund an army to make my abusers' life impossible. I simply disappear and leave.

Hence, as I know I am an eagle, a horse and a wolf, I think you understand that I know very well who I am, that I don't doubt where I go or what I want in life. It is simple, what I want in life is NO ABUSE, NO MISTREATMENT, if you follow that you will get along with me and I won't leave.

To activate the arborescent thinking regarding our conscious decisions made from our soul and spirit, I think it is good to analyze 'the jungle of souls'. You will see that some of them make conscious decisions, and there are others where it is difficult for them to make conscious decisions, like the "duckling" soul (*duckling* meaning "novice" or "clumsy").

I want to tell you that we all have a little bit of all of those souls, in other words, we all have a duckling inside of us that will be apparent some days more than others. That's why we must have some empathy, we are human, we are not perfect and we can make mistakes. **But I promise you that I would never ever make you suffer through a surreal scene with abuse in any form.**

Let's look at 'the jungle of souls':

The parasitic souls: I have seen people who are like ticks, bedbugs, or fleas... people who live at the expense of others or who are bothering others round the clock, offending them or getting offended all day long. Simple fleas.
Hippopotamus soul: gulping down so much, but mainly is a big mouth; I have sinned too in being a big mouth sometimes, but I have also managed to become the powerful bear.
Crocodile soul: you don't see him coming, but when he catches you, he catches you real good. He then executes the death roll with your pain and doesn't stop until he tears you down.
Rhinoceros soul: people that just move forward like donkeys, they are like talking to a wall, just minding their own business, without listening.
Pig soul: they get lost in their own desires; I know perfectly well that you may have encountered some 'piggies' in your life.
Dog soul: man's best friend, but sometimes gets frightened. I prefer the wolf soul who operates on our same frequency so we can understand each other better.
Tiger soul: pretty aggressive people, with an attitude that screams "I am here and I am better than you", I usually take them down a peg or two to make them humbler because if they continue, they will become a Lyonel!
Giraffe soul: they look at you over their shoulder, I consider them people lost in gossiping, in sensationalism, gossip programs and tabloids where everyone looks to others over their shoulder.
Zebra soul: they receive all the attacks and hits, like they don't usually defend themselves or can't defend themselves, they are very passive people and even quite sheeple.
Squirrel soul: these people don't usually interact, the people who were so shy in class that never rose their hand, they go unnoticed, they are not bad people, but they don't act either...
Sloth soul: I am sure that you know some very lazy people, like a groundhog, they are masters in doing basically nothing. I prefer that they do nothing than do evil.
Parrot soul: they never shut up; they are real parrots who I would tell to practice silence. On top of that, most of them don't even listen, and tell you that you are not listening...
Mole soul: they can't see anything, they go underground... they get into here and there...
Ostrich soul: people that don't face their problems or their fears. I find them so repellent. They usually

vibrate in fear and don't even want to see it.

Snake soul: you can see them coming, but when they attack you, you discover they were full of poison because it stayed inside you for days, months or years, depending on how much inner work you have done.

Sheeple soul: most of the population: TV says "A" and all of them repeat that same thing without having the slightest critical thinking. Squared-headed people who are simply ignorant.

Cat soul: they are very sensual and pretty girls, and they are one of the best things in life. The problem is if they also have a pig soul, snake soul and ostrich soul. I know there are good women.

Chicken soul: people that do anything to stop injustice, they just stand aside and won't say a thing, cowards, also I find them very repellent. (They are the opposite of the wolf soul)

Little bird soul: they are very free people, they don't mess with anyone, but when someone messes with them, it can almost destroy the little bird. They are so tiny and weak-hearted...

Gorilla soul: they are good until someone pushes their buttons, you can really feel the potency of a gorilla. I am sure that some of your friends have a gorilla soul.

Shark soul: I really don't understand people who came to this Earth just to bite and bite and make people bleed so much. They only know how to attack and offend others.

Snail soul: very slow people, mentally and emotionally slow. You feel them slowing you down. I can have certain empathy towards them, but if they don't learn fast, I usually leave.

Turtle soul: they have a fierce resistance, people with 'magical powers' because when they are attacked, nothing happens. How can they endure so much and handle it so well?

Bull, bison or buffalo soul: straightforward and direct people, rough people that can handle anything no matter what, they have lots of power.

Fox soul: what they really want from you is not what you think, we can say that they are a little bit fake with ulterior motives.

Vulture soul: people that are just 'around', flying around in the clouds, but when there is a victim, they come down to prey on it. They don't have a second thought when attacking and feeding on it. Parasitized by archons, absolutely.

Rat soul: I am sure that at some point you have said "How can someone be such a rat?"

I think that by setting so many examples of types of souls, you now know what I am referring to. We really are so different because of this. For one reason or another, whether from personal experiences, or social programming, some of us have developed more than others. That's why we don't understand each other, because we are all so different. For me, I have now reached a point where I need the people who surround me to give me mental orgasms, or emotional orgasms, or energetic orgasms. I am not at all talking about the physical body or what happens between the sheets, I am saying that at this point I need people with a certain level of piloting and managing of the mental body, the emotional body and the energetic body, because if not, I will end up totally bored. Well, actually, it is not a need, because myself alone is enough for me, I remind you that I am a lone wolf.

All of this is ´soul´ programming, social programming. **Soul, mind,** memory, experience. **Soul, heart,** feel, experience. **Soul, energy,** moving, flow.

The spirit has everything as standard, it doesn't need anything or anyone, it is the light body. Remember though, that is still good to train the physical body, as I do with martial arts.

So it is important to know, that everyone on a mental level has completed a certain number of flight hours (experience and practice), and this goes for everyone on an emotional level, energetic level, physical level and spiritual level. This is why each of us has developed a completely different soul. It is true for example that I get along with gorilla souls, as well as turtle souls, little bird souls and sloth souls…

This is why we don't understand each other. I need a high level, **because if people go wasting my time, or even worse, they make me endure surreal situations or satanism, I just simply leave… I am doing well by myself!!**

* YOU CAN ONLY DELIVER YOUR MESSAGE TO THOSE WHO VIBRATE IN THE SAME FREQUENCY AS YOU*

SOME SIMPLY CAN'T HEAR YOU,
EVERYTHING IS ABOUT ENERGY FREQUENCY AND VIBRATION

21 ¿HOW TO FIX YOUR PROBLEMS?

This is one of my favorite topics, because many people, especially men, react like this: when a woman (such as the one in red in the Matrix movie) comes to a man to explain her problems, they become so confident and turn into Captain America like "Here I am, I will save you"... parasitism by lyonels... After that they realize that the woman was lying about almost everything, but hey... I wanted to set an example of a tormented soul.

I remember, in Logroño, this happened once to us... A female friend told us a tragic, personal story, and right away, we got into our cars to find and kill her boyfriend. I see now that we were being parasitized by lyonels and archons because we really wanted to kill him, seriously!. Then it turned out that the story she had told us wasn't the full truth...

So, since then, I learned that we all have problems and it's better to let everyone fix their own ones. If we try to solve other people's problems, we will just find ourselves involved. We could call this an organized gang of the subconscious.

When outsiders come to you to explain their problems, be careful. Most of the time they are manipulative people and they omit many details of the story... I find it peculiar because I have never been like that, I have always fixed my own problems. I do not go turning people against others. Notice to the extent people can manipulate others, to the point of making a group of people turn against a single person. Can you see the dishonor and cowardice?
Seeing this from the energetic plane, there are people that contaminate other people's present , this is insane, and they don't realize that this is all about ego, and produced by an unleashed emotional subconscious and their offended little heart. This is one of the ways bullying and harassment starts.

Keep away from the tormented souls that are overly self-conscious, those that suffer and appear damaged. The only cure they can find is inside of them, working on their microcosm and getting rid of their mental and emotional scourge; only by doing this, they will be able to evolve. However, they don't work on it, they are slaves to those beings in other planes that handle them through the pineal gland and enter them through intrusions. At the end of the day, they are a bunch of childish infants...irresponsible people that **do not take the reins of their own life.**

If you hurt me, I get my stuff and I leave, that's it. I disappear, I do not make a fuss, no gossip, no theatrical plays, I don't make a fool of myself, or try to start a gang against you...

Plus, these people, who get themselves into trouble, deserve to have these problems. Look out for yourself and don't go around trying to be a savior. It is better to focus on your subconscious, which has enough problems of its own, rather than worrying about other people's problems and subconscious...

We must see that there are two types of problems: inner problems and outer problems.

The intelligent one: solves the problem
The wise one: avoids the problem
The dumb one: provokes the problem
The dumber one: provokes the same problem more than once
Honestly, I am more of the ´avoiding of the problem type´ and leave without doing anything.
I am also the "maintain my position" type, I stand my ground, like a wolf.

If you have a problem and it has a solution, why do you worry?
If you have a problem and it doesn't have a solution, why do you worry?

At the beginning it is easy to say, but hard to apply. The first time I read those questions was at a Taekwondo class many years ago, and I have remembered ever since. I have not just remembered them, but also I´ve been thinking about them, and taking action based on their principles. If you don't apply them, you will suffer from your problem and from the worry. This can result in you fanaticizing in a loop, which is this limiting pattern of the subconscious. I think we should be more responsible and stop singing along to blood's tune, stop singing along to sorrow's tune and stop singing along to humiliation's tune.

We must shine in states of lucidity vibrating inside us in the present.

If I have a problem with you, this must be resolved just between you and me, for our honor, without anyone meddling in our business; and if necessary, we can "take it outside". Many people live in fear, so they seek help, but then it ends up with six people against one, which is total dishonor.
Besides, it is interesting because these cowards who use people to deal with their problems, to wage their wars, get you involved and just waste your time. It is essential to detect the time-wasters...the sad souls, the souls in torment who are masters in witchcraft.

We must recognise who nurtures us the most, or what nurtures us the most. That is the key. However, stay away from do-goodism and the new age, because if you lend a helping hand to a soul in torment, it will contaminate you, because you won't stop dealing with complaints, hardships, ego, etc. What I promise you 100% is that they will never tell you the whole truth, plainly and transparently; they will always tell you what they want so you take their side, it´s quite sad really. They are very manipulative people. Be careful with half-truths, they are the worst.
That's the best question to ask tormented people suffering from hardship, how much are they hiding?

If my cousin or brother come to me telling me their problems, I am already thinking that he probably deserved that problem and most likely, I won't help him. That's me. However, if it's a serious or a very serious problem, then I can give full rein to my lyonels. I say this, because there are some people who don't know each other at all, they just know each other from the internet, they are complete strangers.

Do you think I would listen to someone who is a stranger to me, that just comes to explain their sorrows...if I don't even do it for my cousin or brother?

The best way forward is to deal with just your own problems, the same as I do - fixing *my* problems, without that urge for gossiping or tabloids, or roumors, or press or celebrity journalism. I'm telling you this because honestly, **I don't like anybody meddling in my problems - I like to be responsible, to face it myself and solve it myself.** I think that is pretty honorable.

Let's be clear, many people on the internet disguise themselves as ´flower-power´, living in their fantasy world, but then stab you in the back like a fox, snake or rat soul. A true human relationship is never possible in a digital world, wake up children! WE ARE MAKING INFANTS OF THE POPULATION.

How can I fix my *own* problems?

This is the question – first you need to detect if they are internal or external problems, I mean, if they really concern you or not. If those problems are from these tormented souls, who involve you in their issues and conduct witchcraft on you, you should pass on their tricks and stories, because those are external problems.

If they are internal problems that really concern you, decide if they are problems of the physical plane, mental plane, emotional plane, energetic plane or the spirit. Well, we now know that the spirit is light, it is complete, it doesn't need anything and I don't think that the spirit will ever have problems.

So study yourself, your inside, delve into the root of the problem and whether it has a solution or not, especially now that you know everything from reading this book. Detect if it due to the subconscious, if they are drainages, in which body is this occurring, if there is a solution. Then act in order to break the limiting pattern, and I will remind you about those ´friends´ that drain us from other planes.

Honestly, people that eat meat, dead cells, blood and transgenics are usually the people who create problems. It is like there is a mini-portal to the astral plane, generated in our stomach, where they poke their hands through, making you easy to parasitize. It is really logical.

They are always ´affected´, and will affect the group.

The following questions would be good for people who have so many problems:

Do you eat a lot of meat?
Do you take a lot of sugar?
Do you have a lot of coffee?

If they answer yes to all of these questions, what happens is not that they have a lot of problems, but instead, they have a constantly ´affected´ life, out of their centers with so many chemicals and dead cells in their stomach. Due to the digestion process, or energetic transmutation, you are what you eat.

Remember, if an archon parasitizes you, you will see it clearly, because you will scream and shout, get angry and infuriated. If a Lyonel parasitizes you, you will humiliate the other party, you are superior, you are god - the other party is the worst thing in the world, you will feel that you are completely above everyone else, and you will communicate that through bad manners and by throwing energetic punches at them. The problem is when you get parasitized by a reptile, because he will execute an expert plan meaning that you will have culminated a plan against the other party. However, you only realise this once it´s too late. You might have the feeling of: "I shouldn't have done that, I should have thought about it more before acting", etc.

If you have a very difficult problem, I advise you to grab a pen and paper and try to open up through it with all your senses. The more you write, the better, let it all out with the following trick:

Method

1) **DEFINITION OF THE PROBLEM (FACTS)**
   Write all of the facts and events that have happened i.e. all the data. <u>Data brainstorm.</u>
2) **SITUATION ANALYSIS (EVOLUTIONARY SEVERITY)**
   Write out the story, including all the information or facts <u>taking their evolution into account</u>. The history.
3) **DIAGNOSIS: MURDER (CAUSE AND CONSEQUENCE)**
   Try to study the reasons (or <u>causes) that brought you to act</u> the way you did, and then the consequences it caused, and even other possible consequences that might had happened due to your actions. You can do this for future decisions too.
4) **ALTERNATIVES (OBJECTIVES)**
   Write down all your objectives and all of the possible alternatives.
5) **ASSESSMENT AND CHOICE (PROS AND CONS OF THE FINAL DECISION)**
   This is similar to step 3, but for the final decision: write down reasons for and against favoring the final decision.

This is for internal problems; for external problems, let other people do it for themselves - let them be open and honest in front of the paper. If you have had a problem that has been draining you for some time already, this is a clue that you should have started this ages ago. If you carry out this method step by step, it means that some people have already crossed the line.

I am like this...if I have a huge problem, I like to write it all down, rather than explaining it to everyone I know, whether they are people from the internet or not. Because if I behave like this, like a tormented soul bothering others, I am acting in a subconscious way, plus, I am contaminating and polluting my present and other people's present. In other words, it is a considerable lack of respect to go around energetically polluting other people with my internal problems. Also, if they are internal problems, the only one that can solve them is me.

Other people won't solve any of my internal problems.
People are so childish with that need to be under someone else's wing, or for other people come and solve their problems. Childish and irresponsible. They make me cringe to be a human being.

We are adults, we should be responsible for ourselves and our own problems. We should be holding the reins of our own lives and not trying to give them to others.

*****The best trick to overcoming overwhelming problems is to record everything…every situation that overwhelms you and seems surreal, get your phone out and record everything, just in case. I do it all the time. For example, I realised how "Agent Smith from Matrix" parasitized a girl who I loved when she was recklessly driving her car. <u>Record surreal moments on your phone, always.</u>

It is simply a case of practicing concentration, conscious breathing and knowing how to vibrate inside of oneself. Specifically, knowing how to vibrate inside of oneself in states of lucidity in the present; not vibrating in the past or in the future, without suffering any kind of intrusion, shining constantly, without reaching euphoria. If you can do this from this physical plane, you can even do it on the astral plane, because they will stop feeding on us if we are lucid or in silence. We need everyone to do this. Everyone should be vibrating inside themselves in states of lucidity without reaching euphoria. Let's not waste energy, damn, don't let them drain us, let them starve in other planes!!

If you invest your time in toxic pursuits and if you nurture toxic people, we will have a toxic world. It is better to focus and nurture only what is really worthy.

IF YOU NURTURE NOURISHING PEOPLE, WE WILL HAVE A NOURISHING WORLD

ABUNDANCE: BE ABLE TO DETACH, SO YOU CAN GIVE

YOUR HEART IS FREE, HAVE THE COURAGE TO LISTEN TO IT

Now that you have read all of this, you can decide if you are an accomplice to this huge energetic drainage, or if you are going to fight side by side with me by taking the reins and responsibility for your life.

YOU ARE NOT RESPONSIBLE FOR HOW THEY PROGRAMMED YOU
YOU ARE 100% RESPONSIBLE FOR FIXING IT

22 LAST WORDS

The number 22 has been following me my entire life. I hope that you enjoyed my book, I have put a lot of effort into summarizing everything as much as possible, so that it´s not too hard to read, so that any lazy guy like me could choose to read a physical book.

Since I have learned all of this wisdom, my life has changed for the better. I don't act as recklessly as before, I think about things more carefully, and especially whether they are subconscious thoughts or not. Before I wasn´t reliable, and now I am, I don't make snap judgements, I'm not as impulsive as I was, and I am no longer so enslaved by my subconscious. I live a freer but also more comfortable life, at ease, without signing any new age etheric contract…I don't ask the universe for anything, I don't ask the sun for anything, or the moon, or the Earth… I don't ask anything external for anything.

If you have been vibrating in yourself in states of lucidity for some time, without etheric contracts and without etheric strings or implants, you can become liberated without even realizing.
When you free your bodies; the physical body, the etheric body and the body of light, you can perform a trick to hack the Matrix. For example, by asking yourself for something, without making any external etheric contracts. If it is something that you really wish for, that you need and want, and you are conscious about it, your body of light can ask your etheric body for it. When you go to sleep, your etheric body will start operating in the astral plane, subconsciously to try and fulfil that wish. I recommend you not to ask for silly things, and to have some respect for all of this…don't go asking and asking like a child. This is just one way to use the etheric body and it is true that this has nothing to do with conscious astral travel.

I don't know if you want me to keep talking about this topic, or if you want some more information about it. If you do, I have a Youtube channel called ´*chemtrails larioja*´ (on this channel, all the videos are worth watching, they won't waste your time). I talk about these topics and many other ones. Maybe you would be interested in passing by and checking it out. Subscribe, watch a bunch of videos and share the good content that I have there…from there you can even get in touch with me and congratulate my work or criticize it. If you have plagued this book with underlining and highlighting and so on, you are like me.
Remember, it is very important that you carefully choose what you watch, what you listen to, what you choose to enter in your life, remember please, that if you choose things that nourish you, we will have a nourishing world. Do as I do, and choose people and things that nourish. And turn your back on toxic people and things.

PS:
If you really want to help me and help everyone wake up, go to Amazon, write LIBÉRATE DE LOS PENSAMIENTOS INTRUSOS (FREE YOURSELF FROM INTRUSIVE THOUGHTS) in the search box, and when you have the link to my book, share it via Whatsapp, Facebook, Instagram, Telegram, email, everything! Close the book, and take some minutes to do so.

It is time for humanity to wake up, be more human, and less abusive, **I wish that we could reach the day where love is lived for real, as conscious love,** without disrespect and without anybody injecting you with fear, doubt or terror.

U.C.C. UNIFORM COMMERCIAL CODE
© ALL RIGHTS RESERVED UCC 1-308 APPLIED ©

INTERNATIONALLY COPYRIGHTED INTELLECTUAL WORK

INTERNATIONAL COVENANT ON ECONOMIC, SOCIAL AND CULTURAL RIGHTS

The 1948 Declaration of Human Rights recognises intellectual property as a fundamental right, i.e. as an instrument that protects the human rights of creators. Article 17, Article 18 and Article 19.

Article 27: The right to the protection of moral and material interests resulting from literary or artistic production if one is the author.

YOUR HEART IS FREE, HAVE THE COURAGE TO LISTEN TO IT

ASK YOURSELF: WHAT WOULD A FREE MAN DO

ASK YOURSELF: WHAT WOULD A FREE WOMAN DO

IF YOU NOURISH THINGS THAT NOURISH, WE WILL HAVE A BETTER WORLD

ABUNDANCE IS BEING ABLE TO LET GO, SO YOU CAN GIVE

VIBRATE INSIDE YOURSELF IN STATES OF LUCIDITY, IN THE PRESENT

SWEATATION BEFORE THE SITUATION AND BE ABOVE THE DRAMA

One of the things about life that surprised me the most

was that I could stop being the old me

and become

a new, different and improved

being.

For the end, I leave you one of my biggest secrets: **THE 'NO MIND STATE'**
This is a state where the conscious is absolute, you can practice it day by day, but mainly I advise you to lie face up on the floor, relax and meditate. Start by relaxing little by little, first of all: the physical body; feet, legs, hips, torso, spine, shoulders, elbows, wrists and head. A very good trick is to focus on relaxing the face; chin, lips, cheekbones, eyes, eyebrows, forehead. Like a candle that melts, do it slowly, and don't forget about the conscious breathing.

Once your physical body is relaxed, go deeper into your mind and physically relax the parts of your brain that you now know very well. You will feel how that mass inside your skull relaxes physically. You can also go to your heart and do the same thing, and of course thank him for keeping on beating. If you want to talk to your heart and open up, this is the perfect moment; remember that when we are vibrating inside of ourselves, we are not making any etheric contract. Most probably your heart will answer you in one way or another and you will make amends with him. You can also contact your energetic body or your body of light, but this is for those who have been already some time practicing the 'no mind state'. After talking to our different bodies, and having relaxed them all, it is time to reach the no mind state.

The goal is simple, being awake but not thinking, in other words, being empty, because when you reach that state you will realize that you are everything, and at the same time you are empty, but you are everything. It is like reaching yin yang, and when you have the smallest thought, the 'no mind state' will break.

At the beginning, some thought will come to your mind, after a while another will come, and then another, and finally you will start thinking about your problems. You have a wild horse inside your skull. But you can domesticate and tame it. Practice this every day and don't give up. Ten minutes should be enough, but the longer you can do it, the better. It is true that the first day you will feel a certain chaos, and you will really have some doubts about if you made it to the no mind state. Focus on the silent spaces, don't focus on the mental trash that may come and distract you, just the silent spaces. If you focus on silence, each time you do it, those spaces will increase in number and duration, day after day of training. You will realize that during those spaces, you are reaching the no mind state.

Actually, it is like a game, where the owner of your life will be decided; will it be you, or that talking subconscious mind who you didn't tell to start thinking but starts thinking regardless of your permission, and in a more brutal way than ever, taking you out of your present, and in fact, stealing your present and stealing your life. I hope that you choose not to be your Matrix slave any longer, like I did.

As the weeks pass by you will see that your mind is not that runaway wild horse like before if you practice the no mind state as much as you can. Bruce Lee cured his paraplegia like this. If your mind focuses on the problem, you will have a problem. If you can be in the no mind state, all of your cells will start to do what they have to do, they will have a certain intelligence.

ADVANCED EPIGENETICS:
An example of advanced epigenetics that caught my attention was a group of monks that practiced several martial arts, and also meditation focused on epigenetics.
They trained the physical body so much, and after, they meditated in silence. After practicing the no mind state to reach high levels of concentration in BETA or GAMMA frequencies, they focused so much on their meditation that they re-lived their training in a very detailed way by being in the THETA state. What happens in these moments is that your mind really believes what they are focusing on, and therefore sends signals and proteins to the muscles so they keep evolving and enlarging.
With time, they stopped doing physical workouts, but they didn't stop meditating in BETA and GAMMA states while exercising. In other words, while meditating, they visualized themselves training in the THETA state. They weren't working out, but they did it so well that they could feel their feet on the floor, feeling the air, feeling their clothes getting wet as they started to sweat, feeling their hair, feeling everything. The more realistic you make your meditation, the more effective it will be. They even felt how every time the push-ups were harder; they had such a high level of visualization, that their brain took it as if it was real.
Well, after some time they realized that by meditating with their mind, their physical body kept evolving, polishing up and refining despite not really being physically active...they did everything with their mind. This is by having the maximum level of concentration in BETA or GAMMA frequencies.
This is a reality that has been occult and hidden from human beings, there is an infinity of possibilities and of arborescent thinking. Each of us can focus on what's interesting for us, and I always say that the focus might be on something that really nourishes you.

In order for you to understand me better, I will explain some of the meditations that I have practiced: you can meditate every day, and after a long time having reached the no mind state, visualize yourself lifting a small stone. The first time it won't be hard at all, that's logical; but every day pick a bigger stone. After a few weeks, visualize that you lift a stone like the ones that Gokul lifted; but you have to do it very well, visualizing that it is really hard for you, that you suffer to lift it, that your veins get bigger with the effort, that your arms get pumped, that your feet sink in the floor... The more details the better, feel your clothes, the air, everything!
I also did this after doing some pull-ups. I lay face up on the floor, relax myself, meditate for a while in the no mind state, and then when I am in a BETA and GAMMA state, I visualize that I go to the pull-up bar and I do some pull-ups mentally. The more real you get the visualization, the more your mind will believe it and the more effect it will have, besides decalcifying the pineal and pituitary glands.
This is advanced epigenetics focused on the physical body, but we could also practice advanced epigenetics in our mind, the emotional body or the energetic body. The infinity of possibilities is a reality. I remember a meditation where I was flying, we jumped from a cliff, and I could absolutely feel the free fall in my body...therefore, if the mind believes it, we have hacked it!!

COLLECTIVE CONSCIOUSNESS:
I know that you believe me, and that everything I have told you in this book resonates with you. You have now understood many things that have happened in your life that were missing a certain name, for example the energetic punches and the drainages. Finally, I want to show you two more stories from this magical world that they hide from us.
Some scientific people went to a pretty big forest. At the north of the forest, they released some

caterpillars that like to eat the forest, like processionary caterpillars. After some time, they went back there and found that the north part of the forest was dead; so they searched for the caterpillars, but they also found them dead. They analyzed the dead trees and the caterpillars and found out that the trees had tried to defend themselves by producing a new toxin that kills caterpillars…however, the caterpillars still ate the north part of the forest. They discovered this because they found that toxin in the caterpillars. They went back to the forest, and continued analyzing, but this time they analyzed the trees that were still alive. In fact, the living trees of the north had plenty of that toxin, but the real surprise came when they analyzed the trees from the east, west and south of the forest. Absolutely all of the trees of the forest had that toxin. Is it possible that some sort of communication between the trees existed like in the movie Avatar? The answer is yes, and still nowadays we don't know if they do it through their root system or through a collective consciousness.

We are not good at being aware of collective consciousness; rather it is a collective subconscious that exists, because everyone is a slave to their intrusive thoughts (I was one more slave to my subconscious, just like you were). But I have faith in this book and that people will share it, it is now or never; either we all wake up at once or we all wake up at once.

Another example of collective consciousness is the example of the hundredth monkey phenomenon. They put several families of monkeys on an island, divided in two parts, north and south. The scientists gave towels full of mud to the monkeys of both the north and the south. One day, a monkey discovered that by soaking the towel in a little stream of water, it changed its color, and each time it was cleaner and cleaner until the towel was almost white. He then started making some noise to inform his monkey partners, so he took another towel full of mud and cleaned it in the water in front of the others to show them. When the towel was clean, all of the other monkeys were surprised and they grabbed some more towels to clean them. As the days passed by, the monkeys in the north didn't do anything and the monkeys in the south had become masters in cleaning towels. The surprise came when that knowledge was activated in the hundredth monkey, like a collective mass. The same collective consciousness expanded that knowledge. After a few days, the monkeys in the north started cleaning towels just like that, as if they already knew it, as if that knowledge was already in them.

My wish is to activate the hundredth monkey phenomenon, with the consciousness program, with the aim of detecting intrusive thoughts and drainages. This would mean all of us becoming better and improved, and therefore being part of a better humanity, a freer one, with less drainages.

Break Free from Intrusive Thougts

www.justiciasocial.com.es

YOUR HEART IS FREE, HAVE THE COURAGE TO LISTEN TO IT

ASK YOURSELF: WHAT WOULD A FREE MAN DO

ASK YOURSELF: WHAT WOULD A FREE WOMAN DO

IF YOU NURTURE THINGS THAT NURTURE WE WILL HAVE A NURTURING WORLD

ABUNDANCE IS BEING ABLE TO LET GO IN ORDER TO GIVE

IT VIBRATES WITHIN YOU IN STATES OF LUCIDITY IN THE PRESENT

SWEATING IN THE FACE OF THE SITUATION AND BEING ABOVE THE DRAMA

I hope you liked the book, I would appreciate a star on Amazon and a comment putting what you thought so I could read them someday, if I see a lot of support I could continue doing more work like this, with information so top. Thanks for giving me the 5 stars :P

WE ARE OF WOLF CODE AND WE PRACTICE HONOR

Printed in Great Britain
by Amazon